Twayne's United States Authors Series

Sylvia E. Bowman, *Editor*

INDIANA UNIVERSITY

Francis Grierson

FRANCIS GRIERSON

By HAROLD P. SIMONSON

University of Puget Sound

 97

Twayne Publishers, Inc.   ::   New York

TO

ERNEST SAMUELS

Preface

DURING the past quarter of a century American literary critics have established a seemingly indestructible hierarchy of major figures. Herman Melville is at the top, or he is there in company with Nathaniel Hawthorne, Henry James, Mark Twain, and William Faulkner. Because these writers speak to our present condition, and because readers go to them for corroboration, no one need be surprised that more and more scholarly books appear about them. The major writers are canonized while many of the minor ones still await appraisal. I do not wish to imply that scholarly examination of major figures should be sacrificed for the minor. Edgar Allan Poe spoke aptly when he said that "laudation of the unworthy is to the worthy the most bitter of all wrongs." Yet I agree with Van Wyck Brooks who argued in *The Writer in America* that what "bodies out a culture" is the "circumfusing variegated bulk of lesser giants."

The American writer Francis Grierson was distinctly such a person. And for this reason he should be better known. By the time of his death in 1927, his works were forgotten—or nearly so. Earlier he had enjoyed considerable publicity with the appearance in London of *Modern Mysticism* (1899), *The Celtic Temperament* (1901), *Parisian Portraits* (1910), *The Humor of the Underman* (1911), and *The Invincible Alliance* (1913). The climax of his eighteen years in London came with the publication of *The Valley of Shadows* (1909), a romanticized account of his childhood in Sangamon County, Illinois, in the 1850's. Readers in 1909 were astonished that Grierson had so successfully re-created the atmosphere of war-clouded Illinois. But despite his achievement in this book, his reputation waned soon after he returned to the United States in 1913. Brooding on the misdirection of a nation given over to the Jazz Age, he recoiled into Spiritualism, a cult which he hoped would awaken people to the folly of their ways. His long career as writer, musician, Spiritualist, and cosmopolite in America and Europe—spanning the years from Abraham Lincoln to Calvin Coolidge—ended in Los Angeles three months before his seventy-ninth birthday.

Only a few critics have paid any attention to Grierson. Theodore Spencer wrote an engaging introduction to *The Valley of Shadows* when the book appeared in a fifth edition in 1948. On this occasion Edmund Wilson wrote a lengthy review for *The*

New Yorker (September 18, 1948), which he enlarged as an important section in *Patriotic Gore* (1962). In 1952 Van Wyck Brooks wrote appreciatively about Grierson in *The Confident Years, 1885-1915,* and then four years later he extended his portrayal of Grierson in *Scenes and Portraits.* Each of these critics recognized a rare quality in Grierson's work, something difficult to define but suggestive of an almost uncanny lyricism. Spencer called *The Valley of Shadows* "a minor classic." Bernard DeVoto, who edited this fifth edition, went a step further by saying, "I should be willing to delete [Spencer's] adjective."

Back in the 1930's Francis Grierson was only slightly better known. The few writers who alluded to him agreed that this enigmatic figure deserved attention. A. R. Orage, the long-time editor of *The New Age* (London), wrote in his *The Art of Reading* (1930): "Somebody ought certainly to make a comprehensive and final study of him. Sometimes I am convinced that he was one of the great charlatans of literature, a writer with nothing original to say, but with an impressive manner of borrowing. At other times I am disposed to give him credit for one of the rarest qualities in literature, namely, atmosphere. . . ." In 1931 Shaemas O'Sheel, former editor of *The New Republic,* tried with little success to re-introduce Grierson's books to the American public. In 1935 Roy P. Basler in *The Lincoln Legend* considered Grierson's *The Valley of Shadows* next only to Winston Churchill's *The Crisis* as a literary work dealing with Abraham Lincoln.

In spite of the fact that these readers thought Grierson's work should be taken seriously as literature, a vague uneasiness about Grierson shaded their praise. Persons who knew him and who read his books, or who listened to his remarkable piano improvisations, thought him a "strange fish." The term, which is Van Wyck Brooks's, suggests the mysterious aura which followed Grierson. Many persons dimly suspected him to be a charlatan, his magnificent aplomb hiding a second-rate mind. His weird music which threaded darkened séance chambers beguiled his audience who, afterwards, wondered if there were not traces of skulduggery somewhere. They marveled at his *savoir faire,* his manner of gaining admission into European courts where he played before royal families and then, after receiving dazzling gifts, disappeared as mysteriously as he had arrived. Something unmistakably decadent yet innocent suggested itself to his friends who saw how, year after year, a certain Lawrence Waldemar Tonner accompanied Grierson everywhere, often waiting for an entire evening on the outside doorsteps while Grierson with rouged cheeks and waxed moustache dined inside with friends. In short, Grierson's career in America and in Europe was such that a person following it is continually touched by a feeling of incredulity.

In this book I have devoted the first three chapters and the final chapter primarily to biographical material. The intervening chapters treat Grierson's "major phase," and thus center upon his social, philosophical, and esthetic ideas during the years from 1889 to 1913 when his chief concern was with writing. Throughout the book I have placed Grierson and his ideas in context with major issues and writers of the time—not to show that Grierson was merely one "who felt that way too" but to show his own uniqueness.

In passing, a word of explanation is needed about Grierson's name. He was christened Benjamin Henry Jesse Francis Shepard and, for short, was called either Jesse or Ben Shepard. When he published *Modern Mysticism* in 1899, he took his mother's maiden name, Grierson, and from that time on he called himself Francis Grierson. Because of this fact, I have consistently referred to him by it even though documentation at times will bear his earlier name.

For this book I have had access to the private collection of Leetha Journey Hofeller of Los Angeles. It contains over two hundred letters formerly belonging to Grierson, an unpublished autobiographical manuscript, and miscellaneous papers. Further primary sources available for my use were at the Junipero Serra Museum of the San Diego Historical Society, the Illinois State Historical Society in Springfield, and the public libraries of San Diego and Los Angeles. To Mrs. Hofeller and the above-named societies and libraries I am indebted. I also acknowledge the assistance given me by the late Van Wyck Brooks, Mr. Carey McWilliams of *The Nation,* and Mr. Jacob Zeitlin. A special word of appreciation acknowledges the enjoyable time I spent in talking about Grierson with Mr. Michael Albert Teleki. I am grateful to Professor A. Kingsley Weatherhead of the University of Oregon for his generous reading of parts of the manuscript; to Professor Harrison Hayford of Northwestern University for his sustained interest in the project; and to my wife Carolyn for all the immeasurables.

H. P. S.

Princeton, New Jersey

Contents

Chronology

1848   Francis Grierson (Benjamin Henry Jesse Francis Shepard) born in Birkenhead, England, on September 18.

1849   Moved with family to Sangamon County, Illinois.

1858   Lived in Alton, Illinois; heard last of Lincoln-Douglas debates.

1859-   Lived in St. Louis and served as page for General John
1862   C. Frémont.

1863-   First discovered his musical talent while living with
1867   family at Niagara Falls; returned to St. Louis, then moved to Chicago where he continued musical study.

1868   Gave musical recitals in New York, Boston, Baltimore.

1869   Went alone to Paris where he enjoyed immediate acclaim as piano improvisator; played in many Parisian salons.

1870   Moved to London to escape Franco-Prussian War; then returned to U.S.

1871   Went again to London, then to Baden-Baden, Cologne, and in October to St. Petersburg, Russia, where he spent the winter and received initial instructions in holding séances.

1872-   In London joined his parents who had recently arrived
1873   from the United States, their homesteading in the Middle West at an end.

1874   In October, held séances with Madame H. P. Blavatsky at Chittenden, Vermont.

1875-   Information about these years extremely scarce. Lived in
1886   San Francisco, Australia, London, Paris, Chicago.

1887-   Built the Villa Montezuma in San Diego where he was a
1889   leading Spiritualist; published his first essays in *The Golden Era;* stayed for a short time in Paris to arrange for publication of *Pensées et Essais* and *Essays and Pen-Pictures.*

1890- Left San Diego and the Villa Montezuma; wandered on
1895   the Continent, meeting artists and royalty and giving
       recitals in Munich, Berlin, Hamburg, Leipzig, Dresden,
       Stuttgart, Karlsruhe.

1896- Settled in London; took name of Francis Grierson with
1913   publication of *Modern Mysticism* in 1899, the first of
       eight books he wrote while living in London.

1913   Returned to United States prior to outbreak of World
       War I; lectured, gave piano recitals, and continued to
       write.

1919   Lectured on Theosophy in Toronto.

1920   Moved to Los Angeles where he lived for the rest of
       his life.

1927   Died on May 29.

Francis Grierson

CHAPTER 1

Early Years in America

AMONG THE MANY American writers who grew up on the frontier and later wrote about it, few are more enigmatic and neglected today than Francis Grierson. It was thought that a fifth edition of *The Valley of Shadows* in 1948 would renew interest in him, but except for Edmund Wilson's review and some reminiscences of Van Wyck Brooks, nothing more was written about either Grierson or his book. Again in 1962 Wilson gave an important place in *Patriotic Gore* to Grierson but, as before, the subject faded out like a lost radio band. Here then is an American writer, dead since 1927, whose life and work tantalize anyone beset with the question of what it is that makes a writer live or die with each successive generation of readers.

I *A Youth on the Prairies*

The story of Grierson goes back to an Illinois log cabin—or even farther back to the English town of Birkenhead, across the Mersey River from Liverpool, where he was born Benjamin Henry Jesse Francis Shepard on September 18, 1848. In March of the next year his parents emigrated to the United States to escape the widespread economic depression which, by 1850, had sent nearly nineteen thousand English settlers to Illinois alone.[1] His father, Joseph Shepard, worked hard on the prairies, though he knew almost from the start that he was ill-suited to this kind of life. Typical of many immigrants from England, he found himself bewildered with the problems of homesteading and with its often terrifying social isolation. That he endured these problems for ten years tells something about his resourcefulness, if not his faith in the American frontier dream. When in 1859 he accepted a government position and moved his family to St. Louis, he had no regrets in leaving behind the log cabin and prairie sod.

How close young Grierson (he took his mother's family name in 1899) was to his father is only partially evident in *The Valley of Shadows*, written in 1909 when Grierson was sixty-one. In this book he portrayed the pioneers, his father among them, as giants who were somehow elemental in their labor. Joseph Shepard appears as a reflective and capable Westerner, strengthened—as Cooper's Deerslayer would say—by living "in the very bosom of natur'." In Grierson's unpublished memoirs written shortly before his death, he remembered his father as "a peaceable man"—quiet, hard-working, and reverent—who made harmony "the dominant note inside as well as outside the house."[2] The impression left in both these accounts by the aging Grierson is that his father once stood in company with the pioneering archetypes. Edwin Björkman, one of the few students of Grierson's work, yielded to the full impact of this image; he called Grierson's parents "shining, winged guardians," Joseph having a "quiet nobility" and Emily, his mother, a "patient kindliness."[3]

Into the portrait of Joseph Shepard, who was Irish by birth, come the lines drawn by Lawrence Waldemar Tonner who was Grierson's friend and companion for over forty years, traveling with him in this country and abroad as a kind of man Friday, Sancho Panza, valet, and agent. Tonner wrote to Grierson's second cousin, General Benjamin Harrison Grierson of the Union Army, that "Jesse's [Grierson's] father is a most awful man in many ways. The whole family live in terror of him.... He is a perfect tyrant over the family ... a good-for-nothing.... Jesse never could get along with him at all."[4] This letter was written at a time when both Tonner and Grierson were financially distressed and, at the same time, unable to pry loose money from either General Grierson or Joseph Shepard. These circumstances undoubtedly colored Tonner's appraisal of Grierson's father. Yet there is sufficient reason to suspect that Grierson's own portrait of his father was a highly idealized one, suitable to the larger image he drew of the frontier itself.

The same can be said about his mother, Emily Grierson Shepard, to whom the Illinois prairies were lonesome and monotonous. Despite her transfiguration in *The Valley of Shadows*, she was no more suited to the rigors of pioneering than was her husband, and it was not until the family moved from St. Louis to Chicago in 1865 that she enjoyed life in America. Out on the prairies it was no advantage that her Scottish lineage included

Sir Robert Grierson, fourteenth Laird of Lag in the fifteenth century, and Sir Robert Redgauntlet of Sir Walter Scott's novel *Redgauntlet*. In writing of these things to her cousin, General Grierson, she noted with pride that many Griersons, including himself, had "figured conspicuously" in history: Constantia Grierson whose writing King George III had praised, Annie Laurie, Major General Wahab of the East Army, and a cousin who "married a Granddaughter of the Indian Prince 'Tippo Taib.'" It is clear that, like Joseph Shepard, she had no regrets in leaving the frontier to others. By 1871, with the prospect of returning to England in a few days, she looked back upon her entire twenty-two years in America as "wanderings in a wilderness," and she encouraged General Grierson to follow them across the Atlantic when his "sojourn amongst the Indians" was over. Writing to her cousin in 1874, three years after her return to "civilized life," she said, "For my part I lost so many precious years of my life wandering in the wilderness."[5]

With his parents, young Grierson also left the frontier. He was eleven when they moved to St. Louis and seventeen when they moved to Chicago. Four years later he was in France, hobnobbing with royalty and artists alike. He never returned to anything remotely resembling pioneer life. He was drawn instead to the cultural and social aristocracy which, especially in England and on the Continent, was frolicking to its end with the expiring century. It is not surprising, therefore, that for his first book Grierson wrote an assortment of fragile essays, in French, entitled *Pensées et Essais*. Published in 1889 when he was forty-one, these Classical *pensées* bear no trace of the American frontier which he had left long ago. Later books—some in French and others in English—had no trace of it either. Then in 1909, removed from the frontier by forty years, Grierson wrote *The Valley of Shadows*, an American classic of frontier literature. As Edmund Wilson has said, it is indeed an odd spectacle in American literary history to find this pale spinner of French essays break out in frontier dialect and rival such storytellers as Mark Twain and Uncle Remus.[6]

Of course Grierson was not the only American writer to have lived on the frontier, left it, and then imaginatively returned to it for literary purposes. One thinks of William Dean Howells who relatively late in life wrote about his Ohio boyhood in such books as *A Boy's Town* (1890), *My Year in a Log Cabin* (1893), and

Years of My Youth (1916). Mark Twain's nostalgia for a youth's paradise returned when, well along with his literary work, he settled in Hartford, Connecticut, to write his long thoughts about youth in his great Mississippi River books. Hamlin Garland followed the same pattern in his four Middle Border novels which recount his boyhood. Grierson is in this same tradition—but with a difference. Grierson's *The Valley of Shadows* was written not only from across the Atlantic but by one who, in his earlier writing, seemed to have severed all his emotional ties with the frontier epic, and among his works which followed there is only scattered frontier flavor. In short, the book is Grierson's single effort to recapture his boyhood and the great national issues surrounding it. Yet it is his most successful book, one which carries its own memorable effects. And those effects make clear that deeply beneath Grierson's other writing, which appears so remote from his Illinois boyhood, there runs a thread of frontier mysticism which he never completely lost.

Unlike his mother, who regarded the frontier experience as precious years lost, Grierson remembered this period as a time when he wandered not in a desolate wilderness but amid "a sea of wild flowers" where close at hand were the strange night noises of prairie birds and animals and not far away the Mississippi River flowing "in one fixed and endless direction."[7] For all his cosmopolitan fancies in later years, he remembered these boyhood times with enduring affection. And more, he infused them with a strange and haunting mystique quite unlike anything written before or since about the war-shadowed garden which was Illinois in the 1850's.

Omitted in Grierson's reminiscences are the familiar activities which boys enjoy. Howells, for example, remembered such youthful fun as marbles in the spring, then foot races, tops, and swimming, followed in the fall by nutting and trapping quail and in the winter by skating. Mark Twain described in detail the activities of his boyhood as acted out by Tom and Huck. There is little of this activity in Grierson's book. Whatever his youthful interests might have been, he wished to suggest to his readers that he distinctly felt as a boy some mysterious correspondence between the visible world and the forces shaping it. The impression is of a boy who is aware that in nature some tremendous reality pulsated. Still more, the self-portrait shows a youth sensitive to the same historic and supernatural forces which disturbed the pioneers who themselves were seen to possess a peculiar wisdom—a power of divination—to interpret the prairie years before the Civil War.

The impressionism in *The Valley of Shadows* can hardly serve as fully accurate documentation for Grierson's early years in Illinois. It is probable, however, that young Grierson did realize a significance of the plains apart from the purely materialistic development of the country or its growth in population and wealth. As a boy too young to be concerned about his parents' economic and social problems, Grierson breathed the prairie and the inexorable river. Observant, sensitive, and meditative, he never forgot them. Björkman said that this early environment "stamped itself on the super-sensitive boy for life,"[8] and other critics have said virtually the same thing. Edmund Wilson thought that what affected young Grierson most in Sangamon County, Illinois, was "the spiritual and even mystical significance of the life there led."[9] "Young as he was," wrote still another critic, "he divined vaguely" the significance of the Illinois prairie and the years spent on it.[10]

All these speculations so dramatically presented in *The Valley of Shadows* underscore the fact that throughout his life Grierson appeared as an indefatigable Romantic. Because of this fact, his writing continually struck an incongruous note when, all around him, came the new voices of Realism. Grierson, a belated Romantic, was a misfit in his day, but he was one who in his recollections of a childhood spent during the ominous years preceding America's most painful conflict wrote poignantly of a national era which even today defies complete understanding.

Living in rural Illinois during the decade preceding the Civil War, Grierson remembered two crucial upheavals close at hand. Both these subjects dominate *The Valley of Shadows,* just as they did his own youth: one was religious, the other, political. That there was a spiritual awakening in the Middle West prior to the outbreak of the Civil War is a generally accepted fact.[11] At Methodist camp meetings pioneers struggled with the devil and, conveniently, found an outlet for their starved emotions. Particularly in Illinois, according to one historian, the sermons flashed with more hell-fire than any that Jonathan Edwards or George Whitefield delivered during the heyday of the Great Awakening; religious tirades by itinerant preachers were often "more psychopathic than the witchcraft mania."[12] Reaction against the Enlightenment of the previous century had erupted, and once again worshipers attempted, as had the earlier Calvinists, to detect sudden revelations of God's power. The frontiersmen looked to comets, earthquakes, storms, and prairie fires as the peculiarly awful language of God. Of Donati's comet, which mysteriously appeared in the skies in 1858, Grierson's Load-Bearer in *The Valley of Shadows* says: "Thar's a mighty power movin' over the yearth" (129). After seeing such signs, the people trembled in the conviction that God was choosing them as instruments in his ineffable plans. This was old-time religion, and natural to it were throngs of clapping, weeping, shouting, moaning, fainting rustics. From his boyhood Grierson remembered the Illinois camp meeting which, he said, was like "a coast strewn with the dead and dying after a great wreck, and a murmuring tumult alternately rose and fell like that from a moaning wind and a surging sea" (*VS,* 150).

Another strong influence in Grierson's youth was the political excitement centering on the momentous question of slavery and on the figure of Abraham Lincoln. In 1858 the Shepards lived in Alton, Illinois, where on October 15 Lincoln and Stephen A. Douglas held the last of their seven famous debates. Young Grierson, who stood close to the front, keenly watched the two men, so strikingly different in word and manner. Years later Grierson described in *The Valley of Shadows* that occasion when, as he remembered, Lincoln "rose from his seat, stretched his long, bony limbs upward as if to get them into working order, and stood like some solitary pine on a lonely summit, very tall, very dark, very gaunt, and very rugged, his swarthy features stamped with a sad serenity, and the instant he began to speak the ungainly mouth lost its heaviness, the half-listless eyes attained a wondrous power, and the people stood bewildered and breathless under the natural magic... (198).

It is clear that Grierson wished to interpret his youth as a time when he not only participated in the crucial events of history but, even more importantly, intuited meaning in them. It was especially in Abraham Lincoln that Grierson found the symbol of American destiny. His prose carries the weight of Lincoln's own mystery, and for this reason Carl Sandburg amply quoted from it.[13] But to even more effect is Grierson's conception of the hero-figure. To young Grierson, the figure of Lincoln loomed awesome enough, but by the time he wrote *The Valley of Shadows* the hero-figure had grown to mythical proportions.

It had grown equally large to millions of Americans to whom hero-worship was nothing new. John C. Frémont was the "Pathfinder"; Andrew Jackson, "Old Hickory"; Zachary Taylor, "Old Rough-and-Ready." But Lincoln was more than even the composite frontiersman. Something mystical and apocalyptic made him appear like another Moses, another Jesus Christ. As Roy P. Basler points out, Americans thought that Lincoln, assassinated on Good Friday, uttered with his dying breath, "Father, forgive them, for they know not what they do."[14] Walt Whitman made this same connection between Lincoln and Jesus in "When Lilacs Last in the Dooryard Bloom'd," as also did Emerson in his eulogistic essay entitled "Abraham Lincoln." Grierson's memory of Lincoln in Illinois helped him to sustain this myth in *The Valley of Shadows*, as well as in a still later work which hailed Lincoln as "the greatest practical mystic the world has known for nineteen hundred years."[15]

Other boyhood incidents made these times especially vivid to Grierson. When the family lived for a while in Macoupin County, near Palmyra, their log house served as a station on the Underground Railway. Grierson's father several times narrowly avoided serious trouble with his neighbors who were strongly sympathetic to the Southern cause. Even more memorable was the April day in 1861 when young Grierson sat in his St. Louis schoolroom and watched the flag of Secession go up. He had earlier witnessed the torchlight parades in St. Louis on the eve of the November election in 1860, a night heavy with fatality. On May 6, less than a month after the shots against Fort Sumter were fired, young Grierson saw Southern troops assemble at Camp Jackson in St. Louis. Four days later he stood on the street as five Northern regiments marched heavily by on their way to Camp Jackson which they easily forced to surrender. That same day he saw a Northern soldier killed by a Southern bullet. He remembered the sight as "indescribably horrible" and his father's words, "this was civil war" (VS, 230). In June he became a page to General Frémont whose headquarters were in St. Louis, and the following year he was close at hand as Northern troops assembled in preparation for their attack upon Vicksburg farther down the river.

All these experiences made their mark on Grierson. Although he left the frontier about as far behind as possible as he wandered among the courts and palaces in Europe, he nevertheless proved in writing *The Valley of Shadows* that nothing could efface those times as a boy when America had both a frontier and a Civil War. Despite all else that *The Valley of Shadows* is, it is a richly moving account of a boy's life in mid-nineteenth-century America in an environment remote from the bustling centers of trade and politics yet strangely close to the deep undercurrents impelling them.

II *Discovery of Musical Talent*

Until Grierson left St. Louis with his family, he had had little formal education. His first school was in Alton where the family lived for a short time when he was ten. Six years in St. Louis allowed for further schooling, but there is no indication that after August, 1863, when the family moved to Niagara Falls, he continued it. In rural Illinois his parents taught him to read and write, their instruction centering mainly upon the Anglican catechism. The only two books Grierson knew as a child were the Bible and the Anglican prayerbook. This fact caused him no regret, nor was he unhappy that the only companions he and his sister Letitia had were grasshoppers, butterflies, squirrels, red-winged blackbirds, and in the evening the whippoorwills, katydids, crickets, and owls. He said many times in later years that he had been fortunately spared formal education before he was ten.

Grierson thought that his early years had provided ideal preparation for what he conceived his task to be. He believed that his peculiar genius lay with art and philosophy or, more specifically, with the search for a singular meaning to nature and history. His impulses often led him into bizarre explorations, in company with the foremost "quacks" and charlatans of his day. Other pursuits yielded rich harvests of music and writing. In all this he remembered late in life that his childhood had been a time that allowed for naturalness and spontaneity. He distrusted education that was overly systematic; and, even more to the point, he distrusted all systems which hampered creative imagination. But, as will be seen, his insistence upon dynamic individualism sharply conflicted with his love of tradition. Both forces pulled at him throughout his life to such an extent that, at the end, his loyalties found expression in the extremes of both.

In looking back over his early years in which formal education

played so little a part, Grierson attributed his own creative
success more to music than to literature. It was at Niagara Falls
that Francis Grierson, at sixteen, first sat before a piano. He had
managed one Sunday to scamper through an unlocked window of
his neighbor's house in which he knew there was a Steinway
piano. Because the owner was away for the weekend, Grierson
was not afraid of being discovered as he sat at the instrument
picking out chords without knowing anything about music: "In
fooling over the keys [he wrote] I happened to strike a full chord,
and I at once realized the influence and direction of something
independent of my intellect and will. . . . Little did I dream when
I awoke to a realization of my hidden faculty on that Sunday
at Niagara Falls of the ordeals attendant on a wandering life
which was to endure as a sort of apprenticeship for more than
forty years."[16]

Before Grierson set out alone for Europe five years later,
relying on his skill as a piano improvisator, he claimed a second
discovery about his musical gifts. When, after thirteen months at
Niagara Falls, the family returned to St. Louis for six months
before moving to Chicago, he one day "upon impulse" visited
the music studio of a Professor Kleber and asked for the teacher's
opinion of his voice. Grierson sang to his own accompaniment.
Extremely pleased by what he heard, Kleber immediately offered
him a place in his choir at St. Xavier's Church. Within two weeks,
Grierson sang at Sunday High Mass a solo part of Haydn's *Ode
to Saint Cecilia* in German. His performance was so exceptional
that the other choir members, reported by Grierson to have been
jealous "at the singing of a young upstart," showed enough displeasure to cause Kleber to assign Grierson to another church
in St. Louis where he could sing without trouble.[17]

In recounting his musical achievements, Grierson strangely
omitted any reference to his sister, Letitia, who, it seems, held
even more promise as a public performer than did he. When
the family moved to Chicago in the winter of 1864, the parents
were hopeful that, by studying elocution, she could have a career
as a public reader. Emily Shepard complained of the high cost
of instruction ($210 for a full course), but she was confident, in
writing to General Grierson, that "there would soon be another
celebrity [*the* family celebrity was the General himself] added
to the family in the person of Letitia" whose performances "will
be a sure fortune for her."[18]

Her brother soon eclipsed her, however, and by the age of twenty he had already set out on his own. He first went to New York, more as an adventurer than as a musician. He took odd jobs only when he immediately needed money. The rest of the time he practiced his music on a rented piano and wandered in and out of social clubs, playing for them upon invitation. On one Sunday in September, 1868, he had "the crazy notion" while out walking to rush into a large hall on Thirty-fourth Street and Broadway just as people were leaving a lecture. He hurried to the piano on the stage and did not lose a second in beginning: "There was not time for a prelude. With an allegro accompaniment, and chords that produced the effect of a piano duet, I attacked high C and held it long enough for the people in the street to stop and listen. In less than two minutes people began to rush back into the hall and continued coming until my audience must have been nearly as large as the audience that had left."[19] At the close of an improvised half-hour concert, a portly man passed a hat for Grierson who walked away with "many dollar bills" in his pocket. From New York he went to Boston, then to Baltimore; there he again made his way by odd jobs and piano improvisations.

A curious detail which later grew to a kind of legend was that Grierson never took piano lessons. He assured his audiences of this fact. When he later became a musical celebrity, he said nothing to alter it. The story stayed with him, and, when critics came to hear him, they happily cited it to make his performances appear more remarkable than they undoubtedly were. Said one critic in *Musical America*: "the boy Grierson went to Paris, where he appeared, without any preliminary instruction either in piano or theory, as a prodigy, giving piano recitals consisting wholly of improvisations.... The young musician did not engage in musical study of any kind, not even in self-directed piano practice, letting his technic grow spontaneously out of his actual improvisations before people."[20] Another wrote: "At twenty-one he was playing before the nobility of Europe—and had never taken a piano lesson in his life! Who was his teacher? He had none. He played because his inner promptings told him he could."[21] The story is easily punctured by Emily Shepard's letter in 1865 to General Grierson. She wrote from Chicago that Letitia "expects to commence reading in Public early in January. Ben [Francis] will go with her and perform on the Piano. He takes lessons of Professor Ansorge and practices a great deal."[22]

The point by itself is not important. With or without piano lessons, Grierson's improvisations were considered to be highly original. Yet his willingness to allow the story to continue that he had had no musical instruction gives a clue to the role Grierson self-consciously wished to play. He wanted to appear not only as a skillful musician but also as a clairvoyant. He wanted to attribute his music to something beyond technical or even imaginative power. Just what this source of his musical power was he never understood, even in his later years, though he claimed that his power welled up from some inner depth beyond the limits of disciplined control. At the age of twenty he began to cultivate this picture of himself, one by which he intended to suggest something ethereal and mystical about his musicianship. At seventy-eight he still thought of himself in this way. For this reason there followed Grierson throughout his career a lurking taint of charlatanry. At the same time, he enjoyed astonishing success as a legitimately skillful artist.

At twenty-one he wanted to go to Paris. He cared little if he had no funds to draw on, once there. What he wanted was the chance to go about "alone in foreign countries" as a kind of wandering minstrel.[23] Eager for adventure, he left in April, 1869, on the *Ville de Paris.*

CHAPTER 2

Widening Interests

I *European Entrées*

WITHOUT MONEY, letters of introduction, companions, or a knowledge of French, Grierson went abroad to see first-hand, he said, the "romantic mysteries of the world" in a country "full of poetry and romance."[1] With a yen for Arabian Nights adventure, he imagined himself the legendary sojourner seeking his fortune and his fame. And blessed with more than usual *savoir faire,* he also wanted to discover just how smartly he could get along in Parisian society.

Writing in his unpublished memoirs shortly before his death, Grierson said that his first impression of Paris failed to live up to his expectations. His earlier accounts indicate, quite to the contrary, that he at once noticed the court splendor of Napoleon III, soon to vanish before the armies of Bismarck.[2] He was also intrigued immediately by the prospect of musical receptions and literary evenings. To young Grierson, Paris unfolded as a rich and full Babylon. He saw nothing to indicate that the Parisian flush was a hectic one, presaging trouble in its social and political world. He later said that when he arrived in France he "was not yet old enough to understand the things that were happening."[3] For nearly ten months there was little to distract him from the indulgence Paris afforded.

What first caught his fancy was the Parisian salon. Its typical bill of fare included piano music, poetry reading, light food, and wine. It was a place where artists, composers, professional critics, and people of fashion came to discuss art and politics. To such an audience, gathered in a quaint old house in the Rue Monsieur, Grierson made his first appearance. Though his piano improvisations failed to interest everyone,[4] they were sufficiently impressive for one guest—Samuel David, a French organist and composer—to exclaim, "C'est extraordinaire!"[5] Soon Grierson was playing in the salons of Mme. de Valois, the Marquise de Ricard, the Comtesse Luigi de Sievers, the Duchesse de la Roche-Guyon, the Comtesse de Beausacq, and the Marquis du Planty; and at each performance he was conspicuously successful.[6] In the 1920's, after Grierson had returned to California for the last time, hand-bills announcing his Los Angeles concerts and lectures hailed him as one who, back in 1869, had become in the short space of a month the musical celebrity of Paris. Arriving unheard-of and unheralded, he was said to have ushered in a new power to musical art. It is true that his reputation as a singer and pianist soon was such that he was chosen by Leon Gastinelle, the composer of sacred music, to sing the leading parts in his Mass composed for the fête of the Annunciation, March 25, 1870, and performed with full orchestra and chorus in the cathedral of Notre Dame. He also sang by special invitation in Saint-Eustache and in the great basilica of Montmartre.[7]

Grierson's friendship with Samuel David provided an introduction to François Auber, at that time an octogenarian who had been Director of the Conservatoire for twenty-nine years. Grierson played for Auber, received an invitation to return, and on the following day after playing for more than an hour, Grierson heard him say to David: "What this young man needs most, like all beginners, is *la pondération.* I advise him to proceed slowly. Whoever tries to control his playing will fail; there is no system by which improvisation can be taught. I hope he will control his art, and not let impulse control him. He should never try to learn; if he does, he may become a conventional pianist."[8]

Soon after his visits with Auber, Grierson was invited to a reception given by Alexandre Dumas *père,* whose words Grierson long remembered: "With your gifts you will find all doors open before you."[9] The prediction proved accurate. Invitations to dinner arrived in such numbers that in dealing with them he requested the advice of friends. One such invitation was to the salon of the Princess Mathilde Bonaparte whose "dark complexion and her large, dreamy eyes of pale gray," Grierson said, made him think of "Zenobia or Cleopatra."[10] The Princess Metternich, wife of the Austrian ambassador, and the Russian Princess Sophia Troubetskoi, wife of the Duc de Morny (half-brother of Emperor Napoleon III), both opened their salons to the young prodigy from America. Within rooms that rivaled the setting of the *Arabian Nights,* he played his piano improvisations. Grierson's desire to wander alone in Europe paid off handsomely during his first ten months in Paris, for during this time he met musical, literary, and social dignitaries who showed him much favor. Regarding his remarkable Parisian adventure, his mother—not a little proud of her son's life abroad—wrote to her cousin, General Grierson, "I wish you could see his medals, the presents and letters from the Nobility."[11]

Grierson would have remained indefinitely in Paris had not the unsettling rumors that the armies of Bismarck and von Moltke were preparing to attack France persuaded him to leave. In April, 1870, Grierson went to London where he stayed at the residence of Viscountess Combermere in Belgrave Square for the next seven months and gave recitals for small but distinguished audiences. Despite his continued success in meeting the right people—such as those who gathered in the homes of Dowager Countess Dunsay or of S. C. Hall, editor of *The Art Journal*—Grierson was not happy in London. Still fresh in his mind were the receptions at the Tuileries and all the elegance of the Champs-Elysées. By contrast he thought London oppressively bourgeois, its social life hardly comparable to that of French salons. It was, then, with regret that he heard the desolate news in September that Napoleon III had been captured at Sedan. Despite what Grierson later saw as the folly of the Second Empire, to him there had been in it an artistic gaiety and flourish which the debacle at Sedan had ended. France was ready for the commonplace of the Republic and for the Realism of Zola. Grierson detested them both.

In December, 1870, he returned home, if it can be said he had one. For three months he stayed in Boston; in April, he went to New York to live with his parents. In that same month he sailed again for Europe, stopping for a short time in London before going to Baden-Baden. Though in retrospect he considered the summer in Baden-Baden "just another experience,"[12] he nevertheless lived at this leading gambling center and fashionable resort in a way not common for a twenty-two-year-old American. Not only did he mix with the opera stars from Europe including Gabrielle Draus from the Paris Opera, but he also fell in with the King and Queen of Prussia, with Madame Viardot-Garcia who was Turgenev's mistress and in whose villa Grierson spent many evenings, and with Helene von Racowitza who was the mistress of Lassalle. The Bishop of Baden also warmly invited him to sing in the Cathedral at High Mass. Grierson sang and played the great organ at the same time, achieving notable acclaim.

Van Wyck Brooks captured the peculiar atmosphere of Grierson's life at this time by comparing him to those musicians of mysterious origin in James Huneker's *Melomaniacs* (1902) who wandered through Europe playing in the old historic salons of princesses.[13] Grierson had taken lessons earlier but now, determined to make his way independently, he sought audiences rather than teachers, inspiration rather than discipline. He grew more serious about the possible connection between music and clairvoyance. And, all the while, he continued his haphazard itinerary which, in the autumn of 1871, took him to the Cologne conservatory of Ferdinand Hiller, who invited him to take part in the concert being held on the day of his arrival by Hiller's students in the Cologne cathedral. "Sure enough," Grierson remembered, "when the time arrived he shoved me forward and I walked up the long aisle to the piano, without an inkling of inspiration. And yet, once there, I had to demonstrate something . . . and judging by the applause which began when I left the instrument . . . the playing must have produced an effect."[14]

He left Cologne for Russia, arriving in St. Petersburg in October with only enough money to pay expenses for one week. Being in a strange city and not knowing the language in no way ruffled him:

> I felt so secure, so much at ease psychically and physically that I spent hours on the divan reading Byron in the first Murray edition presented to me by a lady in Baden-Baden the previous summer. Instead of walking about the city looking at the sights, I sat in my large, comfortable room, as much at home as if I had owned it. My thoughts were of Byron. I was steeped, not in the civic and social aura of Petersburg, but in the atmosphere of Byronic adventure, and I remained in this mental condition for six days, secluded from every exterior influence.[15]

On the seventh day he presented a letter of introduction to a Madame Hardy from her sister in Paris. He was taken in by Madame and Monsieur Hardy, owners of the luxurious Restaurant Dusseau in St. Petersburg, and in their home he spent the winter months, "crammed with pleasure and amusements of all sorts" when "life began at half-past eleven and continued until four or five in the morning."[16] He met Hortense Schneider, the Parisian singer, at a reception given for her by Alexander II. Through an introduction by Princess Abamelik, Grierson also met the Russian mystic, General Jourafsky, who instructed him in conducting séances. In the spring, Grierson visited the imperial palace which he described in his essay "Impressions d'une Visite à Gatchina" in *Pensées et Essais* (1889). The czar was not then in residence, but Grierson returned a week later to play for him.

The winter in Russia brought Grierson as close to the immemorial East of mysticism as he ever came. In his own development, the visit to Russia served to enlarge his occult interests and, one supposes, his own secret powers which occultism purports to nurture. His remarkable success in music and social free-wheeling seemed to verify what to him was obedience to his "impulses." And now, with the new possibilities before him to combine music with these esoteric impulses, especially in séance chambers, Grierson was ripe for the many influences of Madame Blavatsky and her teachings. Her gospel would particularly suit Grierson. The way she ingeniously streamlined the mystical yearnings of Eastern religion would satisfy his demand for tangible results, and in her doctrine of theosophy she would reassure him of his own capacity to reach theosophic wisdom—literally, the wisdom of the divine. Questionable as her techniques were, she persuaded many American intellectuals to believe in her. And under the sway of her uncanny methods Grierson was soon to fall.

In the summer of 1872 Grierson moved from St. Petersburg to London where he met his family, now back in England after their long "wilderness" experience in America. Madame Blavatsky at this time was a medium in Cairo. In July of the following year she landed anonymously in New York. During that year, 1873, Grierson remained in London; but in September, 1874, he returned to New York and in October was in Chittenden, Vermont, a visitor at the home of two farmers, William and Horace Eddy. Madame Blavatsky had arrived there from New York only a few days before.

II *Musicales and Séances*

It is important to remember that around this time many writers were turning to Theosophy as a rationale for their artistic commitment. In the 1880's both William Butler Yeats and George Russell took it up. Edwin Arnold's *Light in Asia* (1879), which in verse handily solved the problem of evil, went through some sixty editions in England and eighty in the United States. Its popularity attested a growing uneasiness about civilization's blessings which all too blatantly were seen as vulgar and materialistic. In seeking a "passage to India," many people believed that in Eastern religion the ambiguities of Western ideology could be reconciled. American novelists such as Howells and Theodore Dreiser dabbled in Theosophy and its claims about the spirit world. Far more serious were the investigations of men like Percival Lowell in *The Soul of the Far East* (1888); William Sturgis Bigelow in *Buddhism and Immortality* (1908); John La Farge (who with Henry Adams fled to the South Seas in 1890) in *An Artist's Letters from Japan* (1897); and Lafcadio Hearn in a long series of volumes dealing with his adopted country, Japan. As Arthur Christy has made clear, many writers of the late nineteenth century thought in terms of Oriental mysticism rather than in those of Western materialism.[17] Grierson was overwhelmingly attracted by the same mysticism, and in time he would write many essays about it. For the present he had found a kindred spirit in Madame Blavatsky, a Russian newly arrived in the United States from Egypt and earlier from Tibet.

Grierson spent ten days with Madame Blavatsky at Chittenden, a small town in Vermont's Green Mountains—"a country," Grierson said, "of bewildering silence and haunting isolation."[18] Gathered with Grierson and the so-called priestess of the occult were "cranks" who came "from far and near to attend the seances."[19] As the center of attraction, Madame Blavatsky made a striking impression upon Grierson.

> Her kinky hair [he wrote in *Anecdotes and Episodes*], her wide, almost flat, nose, and thick lips, harmonized well with her swarthy skin. Her movements were languid and slow. She never smiled, nor did she ever display a sense of humor. Her dress was ill-fitting, the fabric colourless, and of a non-descript character. The two things about her that attracted my attention were her slovenly appearance and her great staring eyes. . . . I saw them a cold, callous grey. They suggested something hidden and forbidding, something between viper and vampire (69-70).

Grierson remembered that, as the days wore on, many visitors were plainly bored. Except for Colonel Henry Steel Olcott, who later became the co-founder of Theosophy with Madame

Blavatsky, the company was not much impressed with what it saw in the séances, held every evening in the large kitchen furnished with a platform which served, according to Olcott, "for the stalking in and out of the 'appearances.' "[20] But Olcott and Grierson were far from bored. In his *Old Diary Leaves* (1895) Olcott reported that up to the time of Madame Blavatsky's arrival at Chittenden the only spooks whom the "poor, ill-educated, and prejudiced" Eddy brothers could produce were "Red Indians, or Americans or Europeans akin to visitors." "But," he soberly continued, "on the first evening of her stay spooks of other nationalities came before us.... It was long afterwards that I was informed that she had evoked them by her own developed masterful power."[21] As for Grierson, the manner of the woman was nothing less than marvelous. After he had finished improvising on the piano, she would frequently step forward, fix her mesmeric gaze on unsuspecting Colonel Olcott, and "with one swift gesture close her hypnotic tentacles on the personality of the man who had neither the time nor the wit to realize what was happening." In language no less weird, Grierson wrote that at Chittenden "the hieroglyphs of Modern Theosophy were written as by an invisible hand on the scroll of the mystical future."[22]

After leaving the farm, Grierson never saw Olcott again, but he visited Madame Blavatsky many times at Irving Place after her return to New York where she continued to hold séances in table-tipping, rapping, and spelling out messages. Despite his frequent visits to her, she was not attracted to him. She wrote to Colonel Olcott within a week after she left Chittenden that he, Olcott, should not praise "the mediumistic musical performance of one Jesse Shepard [sic], whose pretense to having sung before the Czar, and other boasts she had discovered to be absolutely false."[23] Just what she had learned about Grierson is not certain. She was convinced, however, that if he were praised by Olcott in Theosophical tracts which were to appear, Olcott would "injure Spiritualism." She made it clear to Olcott that she wished to save the cult from the danger of what she called charlatanry, immorality, and triviality.

She had apparently learned at least two facts leading to her distrust of Grierson. He had brought her many of his St. Petersburg credentials, in Russian, to translate. Among them was a police license to sing at the Salle Koch which she disparagingly described to Olcott as a "low lager-bier [sic] saloon and dance hall, resorted to by dissipated characters of both sexes."[24] She also told Olcott that Grierson had paid thirty-two roubles to a music-master "for *teaching* [my italics] him certain Russian songs —which we heard him sing at Eddy's, *in a dark seance when he was ostensibly under the control of Grisi and Lablache!"* [her italics].[25] Grierson had duped them at Chittenden! Oblivious to her own pretensions, she had detected charlatanism in Grierson. She told Olcott that she regretted ever having met Grierson. In language fitting to her calling, she said he had been led to her by "his unlucky star."

Grierson's activity for the next fifteen years is difficult to trace. After his visits with Madame Blavatsky in New York he went west, turning up in 1875 in San Francisco where he first had the opportunity to study the Chinese, an interest which much later crystallized into fear of the "yellow menace." The only other clue to his activities in California at this time is his account of a piano recital given in a mining village near Sacramento. The piano which was provided him had several broken strings; but, typically unabashed, he managed to make weird music imitating a Chinese orchestra. His performance ended with a storm of applause—"Some laughed with glee, some shouted, and some emitted Indian yells that pierced the ceiling."[26] In 1877 he sailed for Australia, spent a year there, and was again disturbed by the threat that the yellow race might overrun this far outpost of Western civilization.

Having in the previous years traveled thousands of miles on three continents, Grierson, now thirty-two, was back in Chicago in 1880, his memory of the Chittenden events still vivid and his interest in the spirit world further excited by his frequent visits to Chicago séances. One medium, a Mrs. H. H. Crocker, allowed him to hold a series of séances in her parlors. These séances are described by H. C. Hensley, who heard about them from a San Diego spiritualist, Hudson Tuttle, whose daughter reported that at Grierson's séances "strange and unaccountable phenomena nightly occurred." She continued, as quoted by Hensley:

> "He was very particular that no more than twelve, or at most, fourteen, persons should attend, charging them $2 each. He seated the members carefully and required them to clasp hands. He tacked shawls over the heavy window-shades and locked the doors himself. The rooms were in absolute darkness. He then explained that he was controlled by a band of Egyptian

spirits, the leader of whom had lived on earth when the pyramids were young, and who gave what was then, and has constantly been, Mr. Shepard's leading performance. After this, he sang in two voices, a feat which has astonished so many listeners, 'sontag' (some spirit-familiar) singing in one voice and the Egyptian in the other. Another 'spirit' accompanied on the harp. Between the musical pieces, Mr. Shepard, 'under influence,' gave tests, describing spirit friends, etc."[27]

His practice was more spiritually than financially rewarding, for his circumstances in Chicago were so depressed that he was obliged to pawn a fur coat, made of three thousand squirrel skins and presented to him, said Tuttle's daughter, "by some duchess (or countess) in Europe." He found sufficient money, however, to go to London again in the same year where he visited his parents and did some lecturing. Later he went to Paris where for the first time he visited Stéphane Mallarmé's salon. Nothing is heard from him again until 1885 when his mother reported that he had been in London the previous summer and that she hoped to see him again during the current summer.

In 1887 Grierson finally struck it rich. For the next two years his finances were secure and his mediumistic triumphs sensational. Among his coterie he was the unrivaled center of attraction. From 1887 to 1889 Grierson and his friend, Tonner, whom he had met earlier in Chicago, lived in a palatial San Diego house called the Villa Montezuma. Freed from earthly worries of money and skilled as both musician and occultist, he now practiced his art of musical séances amid surroundings no less exotic than those of the French salons.

III *Charlantanry in San Diego*

It is with his activities in San Diego that one finds an astonishing record of experience. Strangely enough, Grierson did not refer to these two years in either his autobiographical essay prefacing *The Celtic Temperament* or in his unpublished memoirs, *Anecdotes and Episodes*. This omission is hardly an oversight, for he enjoyed in the Villa Montezuma the kind of splendor and fame which perfectly suited his inclinations. Tonner was similarly reticent. His only published reference to San Diego and to the house in which they lived appeared in an erratic monthly newspaper called *Boston Ideas*. Tonner wrote: "The house that Mr. Grierson built was called Villa Montezuma and it is at the corner of K and 20th Street." After giving a brief description of the house, he continued: "Certain rich townspeople gave the land and some of the money to build the Villa, the idea being to attract attention to the town (which it certainly did)." He listed some of the well-known persons who visited them (Joaquin Miller, General Grierson, Governor Robert W. Waterman and ex-Governor John G. Downey both of California, and others); then Tonner concluded: "When the boom died out in San Diego in 1889 we had to sell for what we could get. We gave half the proceeds to those who had supplied the money, which they considered quite generous, for it was not necessary to return any, and the following year we went to Europe and Jesse Shepard began his literary career in earnest."[28]

Both Theodore Spencer in his introduction to *The Valley of Shadows* (fifth edition) and Edmund Wilson in *Patriotic Gore* accept this account as complete. Grierson's own silence about San Diego and Tonner's incomplete facts clearly suggest that more went on than either person wanted known and than has been assumed since. Confident that his séances would attract large audiences, Grierson regarded San Diego as an ideal place for a newcomer to play his game. He arrived at a time when Southern California was enjoying unprecedented prosperity with the completion in 1886 of the Atchison, Topeka, and Santa Fe Railroad, which broke the Southern Pacific monopoly. The heart of the most exaggerated aspects of the new prosperity was San Diego where, according to historian Franklin Walker, "50,000 people tried to get rich in a week."[29] And so, with questionable motives, Grierson set out to test his charm upon the credulous Californians.

The citizens of San Diego were immediately impressed by Grierson who, as "a man of rare charm and highest culture,"[30] had seemed to arrive from nowhere. Mrs. Vine Bowers, a mere girl at the time of Grierson's arrival, later remembered from accounts of her mother that Grierson—"famous (or infamous)"— had had a striking personality and appearance: tall, slender, dark, and artistic-looking. His hands were long and slender, with incredibly long fingers, and he played brilliantly on the piano. But, as Mrs. Bowers recalled, "his music was a medium to pave the way for his real purpose—easy money. And the way to that end was Spiritualism."[31]

Spiritualism, at fever height all over the country in the late 1880's, had an especially active following in San Diego. The leader was Mrs. Elsie Reynolds whose prowess only Grierson could eclipse. He lost no time in obtaining the admiration of two brothers, William and John High, who as wealthy cattlemen had been fleeced of their property and cash by a group of Spiritualists whose trickery had succeeded in getting the two brothers to donate money for the advancement of the Spiritualist movement. Their money gone, the Highs left their ranch and came to the city where they once again gained considerable wealth in a fruit and produce business. But the virus of Spiritualism was in their veins, and Grierson, an expert, soon had them in his control. Through spirit messages, hypnotism, or whatever, he persuaded them to build him the mansion—and to furnish it with exotic imports. Sam High, a nephew of the High brothers, told the story this way:

> Yes, I remember Jesse Shepard. . . . I remember him well and a fine fraud he was. . . .
>
> I remember when this house was going up everybody was talking about it and wondering who was building it. I myself had no idea until one day when I was talking to Uncle William I asked him if he knew and he said to me: "Well, I'll tell you. It's me and my brother." That's all he said and I asked him no questions.
>
> Later on people began coming to me and telling me that it was a shame the way Shepard was getting money out of my uncles and that I ought to get everything from them I could; that they would need it later on. But I figured that they were grown men with more experience than I had had and knew their own business. . . .
>
> Long after Shepard had gone, long after Uncle William died, I was sitting alone with Uncle John one night when I turned and put it right to him.
>
> "Uncle," I said, "it was hypnotism and nothing else. That man had us so hypnotized that we would have done anything under heaven he told us to."
>
> He certainly was a peculiar genius. I never understood how he worked it, and I guess no one else did either. . . .
>
> Sad as it was in one way, I can't help laughing . . . to think of Shepard with his secretary [Tonner] and servants, rolling in luxury, and the two poor uncles, who were putting up for it. . . .[32]

These accounts of Mrs. Bowers and of Sam High contrast rather significantly with Tonner's statement. High went on to explain that Shepard (Grierson), who had become acquainted with the two brothers through E. W. Hulburt, a local Spiritualist, gave them messages purporting to come from the spirit of William's deceased wife. These messages instructed them to build a monument in her memory, but all plans for it were to be left in Grierson's hands. The Highs mortgaged their holdings and financed the house. Grierson and Tonner lived in the mansion until the High money ran out. Then they disappeared as mysteriously as they had arrived.

The most complete description of the Villa Montezuma is found in T. S. Van Dyke's *The City and County of San Diego* (1888). When Grierson occupied the place, each room had a different kind of wood paneling. Throughout the house were deep rugs, heavily jeweled *objets* and candelabra, life-sized busts, and stained-glass windows. In the drawing room, for example, was a bay window eighteen feet deep, of bent glass, the upper sashes containing in art glass life-sized heads of Shakespeare, Goethe, and Corneille. The ceiling was silvered and bronzed, relieved by deep panels of redwood. The stained-glass windows in the music room were especially exquisite and the walls even more ornate: the hard-finished redwood was relieved by ebony panels inlaid with bas-relief figures of ivory and mother-of-pearl. An elaborate Oriental candelabrum hung from the ceiling, and on the highly waxed floor were six heavy Persian rugs with an immense polar bear skin in the center. On the second floor were several rooms, one of them containing ten windows of irregular form overlooking the mountains to the east, Mexico to the south, and the ocean to the west, with the Coronado Islands and Point Loma in the distance. A Spanish cedar stairway led from this room to a turret-like observatory directly above. From without, the house resembled a feudal castle with its several turrets, its darkened windows, and its roof of black walnut shingles.

What went on within this house Grierson never told, except to say in a letter to General Grierson that he never attempted music "in the day time."[33] Tonner was equally noncommittal. Yet it is no secret that Grierson held private musical séances. Amid an opulence which was muted or, perhaps, intensified by dark wainscoting and stained-glass windows, Grierson enthralled his guests with unearthly chords and melodies. Some persons claimed to have heard drums, tambourines, and trumpets sounding all over the room and voices coming from trumpets. Other guests reported hearing choirs of voices led by Grierson's own soprano voice which soared among the higher notes, then by his bass which some said was "as grand and melodious as it was magnetic." The effect on most was "simply indescribable!"[34] Even Sam High, who professed firm opinions against the possibility of spiritual manifestations, confessed attendance at one of Grierson's musicales. He said he was "contemptuous" at first about the whole mysterious business but afterwards felt that the experience had been "one of the most wonderful" in his life.[35]

Grierson was not long in San Diego before his interest in writing equaled that in music. In June, 1887, just two weeks before the Villa Montezuma was completed, he wrote to General Grierson, "I shall let music take a second place in the future, as I wish to do a great deal of magazine and book work."[36] His musical séances were, however, more important to him than this letter indicates. Nevertheless, his literary ambitions were awakened; and in June he published his first essay in *The Golden Era*, a sturdy West Coast journal which carried much of the early work of Bret Harte, Mark Twain, and Joaquin Miller. By April of the following year five more essays had appeared in the same magazine.

In the autumn of 1888 Grierson and Tonner left San Diego for Paris, not returning again until September, 1889. It is no mystery why they went: Grierson wanted to negotiate for the publication of his collected writings. In the spring of 1889 two books were published, *Pensées et Essais* and *Essays and Pen-Pictures*, both containing several of the same essays which had appeared earlier in *The Golden Era*.

Grierson was back in San Diego in September. The congratulatory letters from certain French readers of his books convinced him that these two volumes would mark the beginning of his literary career. His financial distress in San Diego also convinced him that to continue writing he would have to leave the Villa Montezuma. Danger of foreclosure was pending for non-payment of interest on the mortgage, and his request to General Grierson for $450 by November 23 brought nothing. A second letter was sent to the general, this time by Tonner, who explained that Grierson was "in such a state of mind that he could neither write nor do anything else," that he was "almost crazy with worry and trouble," and that he had "only $10 in his pocket."[37] The general sent no money, and their request to Joseph Shepard was equally fruitless. Furthermore, the High brothers had no money to lend. But because the Highs still retained an interest in the property, Grierson figured that, if he could persuade the brothers to trade the Villa Montezuma for income property known to him in Cheyenne, Wyoming, he might extricate himself. The Highs were taken in by Grierson's maneuver, and Grierson quickly left. The deed to the property for which the Villa had been traded came to the Highs, who learned that the property was only an abandoned shack earlier used as a country store. Even the land on which it stood was valueless.[38] Not heard of again in San Diego, Grierson left behind the California Spiritualists who could only wonder what had happened. As for Grierson, he wanted to renew acquaintances with some of the French writers and celebrities he had met earlier. He also wanted to begin a serious literary career. In the summer of 1890 he and Tonner arrived in France for the start of a continuous twenty-three year residence abroad during which time Grierson established his literary reputation.

CHAPTER 3

Literary Achievement

S AM HIGH'S SUMMARY of Grierson's two-year show in San Diego is as good as any: "Sad as it was in one way, I can't help laughing...." With satin touch Grierson had hoodwinked the Spiritualists, particularly William and John High. No one questioned his skill in *this* performance. A more subtle question concerns his motives: Was Grierson a charlatan out for his own advantage? His San Diego exploits leave little room for doubt. Yet, as Sam High remembered, Grierson was also "a peculiar genius."

After a certain point, charlatanry and genius go their separate ways, though admittedly there can still be confusion about the meaning of the two words. With Grierson, the nagging question arises again and again: Was he a charlatan or not? Van Wyck Brooks observed that Grierson possessed a "curious innocence"[1] which, like the quality of genius, strikes one as hardly compatible with charlatanry. In his book *The Art of Reading* (1930) A. R. Orage flirted with the question of Grierson's charlatanry and came close to an affirmative answer. Edmund Wilson also raised the question and concluded that, while Grierson was "unquestionably" an enigma, he was no charlatan—"or not consciously and intentionally one."[2]

It is clear that Grierson took himself seriously. His belief in the supernatural power of music had an unmistakable earnestness. By itself, earnestness of course does not preclude gullibility or downright fakery; but, when it is coupled with trust—viewed as a decision for the ultimate character of reality—then it may qualify belief in a manner one is reluctant to belittle. Grierson's devotion to music and later to writing reflected this peculiar quality which also underlay his commitment to certain ideas. And because these ideas bear the sporadic marks of genuine sophistication, his writing deserves attention.

I *Germinal Ideas*

The substance of his six essays written for *The Golden Era* points to themes he enlarged on later.[3] As would be expected, he drew upon his travels in Europe and his musical performances in Parisian salons. Of more interest are his germinal ideas regarding the spirit world, his criticism of contemporary culture, and his views on art.

In these essays he made his position clear that all events in art, religion, and even politics are related to a higher law which scientific inquiry can never explain. Despite the inscrutability of this law, Grierson believed that intimations of it are perceptible to artistic geniuses who have first freed themselves from the tyranny of mechanistic principles and empirical methods. Furthermore, he thought it wrong to assume that the mind in its pursuit of truth is wholly dependent upon reason or intellect. Such dependency would stifle creative art which, for Grierson, included his own genius for musical improvisations. The key issue for Grierson was simply that if the artist succumbed to scientific positivism (his examples were Emile Zola and the American realist, E. W. Howe), he would lose his place as demi-god, as a mediator between the worlds of spirit and of empirical fact. Like the Romantics who preceded him, Grierson believed that a strict reliance upon observation rather than upon fancy and imagination spelled the death of art. All this was Grierson's early hue and cry which echoes again and again in his later essays.

The six essays attracted only limited attention, though several California reviewers thought that Grierson's literary faculty equaled, if not surpassed, his musical gifts.[4] These essays show a stylistic characteristic—the use of aphorism—which he later developed with more precision. By means of a severely aphoristic style he hoped to give the impression of spontaneity consonant with what he considered to be his own manner of thinking. The result in these essays is often vague generalizations couched in swollen imagery, such as in the following example: "the poetic clouds of illusion and romance have been tapped, the springs of rhythmic mystery have run dry, the prismatic fountains of poetic license have ceased to flow."[5] What all this means is difficult to ascertain, but somewhere in the welter of language is Grierson's conviction that writers no longer inhabit Mt. Parnassus.

The two books Grierson went to Paris in 1889 to publish—

Pensées et Essais and *Essays and Pen-Pictures*—contain more of these curious essays in which aphorisms sometimes barely rocket off the ground. Each book includes essays appearing also in the other, as well as several essays previously published in *The Golden Era*. The newly added ones recounted experiences at Baden-Baden in 1871, his 1872 visit to the Palace of Gatchina in Russia, his interview with Alexandre Dumas *père,* and his observations on Parisian aristocracy of the Third Republic. Some literary criticism appeared in essays on Byron and Carlyle, on Shakespeare's *Macbeth,* and on the life of Joseph Roux.

The most important essay in *Pensées et Essais*—the first of these two books—is "La Révolte Idéaliste."[6] In it he attacked French literary Realism so unremittingly that even in his omission of Zola he leaves little doubt that this French novelist was the literary archvillain. Grierson charged that a "typical realist is stupidly vulgar, unable . . . to come up to the realm of the poetic, the imaginative, and the beautiful." He did not deny the realist his power, but to Grierson it was "power without poetry, strength without devotion, passion without sympathy." The effect, he said, was of an "opium pipe which captivates and then stupefies."[7]

In this essay Grierson set himself squarely against the Realism of his day. Of course he was not alone in this position. In France there were Arthur Rimbaud, Stéphane Mallarmé, Charles Baudelaire, Leconte de Lisle, Edmond Rostand, and Pierre Loti (Louis Marie Julien Viaud); in Germany, Stefan George and Hugo von Hofmannsthal; in England, Oscar Wilde and the Pre-Raphaelites; and in America, Lafcadio Hearn, James Branch Cabell, Edgar Saltus, and James Huneker. But Grierson came close in this essay to disavowing *any* literary approach which limited the writer to observable facts and thereby denied him access to the ideal world of spirit. Despairingly, he asked in "La Révolte Idéaliste" if it is any surprise that people who have been reduced to pawns and subjected to scientific analysis now turn toward India to find help.

The most important and in some ways most baffling essay appearing in his other book, *Essays and Pen-Pictures,* came close to contradicting his own spiritualistic practices in Chittenden, Chicago, San Diego, and elsewhere. "For the first time in ages," he wrote in "Phenomenalism versus Culture," "we have the sad spectacle of science aiding and abetting a system of spiritual magic, analogous to the practice of medieval black art. Eminent men, under the peculiar illusions of sights and sense, countenance and applaud the freaks and follies of certain psychical performances."[8] Grierson wrote other such statements of dissatisfaction about the cult with which he associated until his death in 1927. But the importance of this early essay is that it shows Grierson's ambivalence about the very thing he dabbled with, became an expert in, and finally committed himself to. In the rage over occultism Grierson recognized the presence of malpractitioners, and he obviously asked himself some searching questions about his own participation. What Grierson was determined to do, however, was to place the practice of spiritualism and all its misty ramifications on a sound philosophical footing. He wanted to make certain that theory counted as much as practice and that the practitioner, meaning himself, was also a philosopher.

Again, it is clear that Grierson took himself with utmost seriousness. His philosophical position during his major period of writing steadfastly avowed traditional idealism. But, once again, the fact intrudes that Grierson did not always succeed in accommodating his practice to precept. In his final years he displayed open ambivalence between his efforts to explain spiritualism and to practice it. His strangest of all books which he called *Psycho-Phone Messages,* privately published in Los Angeles in 1921, was a pathetic effort to give philosophic credence to a make-believe gadget which supposedly transmitted psychic messages from the dead. In Grierson's writing from beginning to end runs this thread—sometimes hardly discernible and other times blatant—of something less than total integrity. The misgivings of Orage, Brooks, Wilson, and others never have quite dissipated, try as one will today to dispel them. Grierson obviously had his own misgivings which his essay "Phenomenalism versus Culture" makes apparent. Ambivalence itself is nothing new. A man's most inward motives are scarcely known to himself, rarely to his closest friends, and almost never to his critics removed in time. Grierson's case illustrates the point. What is of interest to the student is Grierson's long effort to reconcile his personal ambivalence and, at the same time, to discover and correct it in the world about him.

II *Books and Reputation*

Between 1890 and the publication of *Modern Mysticism* in 1899 Grierson wrote comparatively little. For the *Nouvelle Revue Internationale* he contributed an article in 1891 that discussed the

Yellow Peril in the East, a theme he developed more fully in 1913 in his *The Invincible Alliance*. He also wrote a series of articles for both the *Nouvelle Revue Internationale* and the *Galignani Messenger* (an English newspaper published in Paris) on the Wagnerian festival at Bayreuth which he attended in the summer of 1891. Wentworth Huyshe of the *Galignani Messenger* asked him to submit other short newspaper pieces the following year. One of them was on Mallarmé, an article that the poet answered in a letter to Grierson. "With this exquisite article," Mallarmé said, "you haunt the home on the Rue de Rome and bring back the memories of the host, such at least as he himself would like to know."[9]

Grierson's scant output at this time indicates no slackening in his literary ambitions. Already acquainted with many French notables, he was now eager to move more specifically into literary circles. He frequented Mallarmé's salon, the center of activity among the French Symbolists. On Tuesday evenings when people gathered at his salon, Mallarmé stood by the fireplace talking in a low voice, half to himself and half to his visitors. He made a striking impression upon Grierson who thought he typified the person freed from the bondage of convention. Another French writer whose friendship Grierson cultivated was Henri de Bornier, librarian of the Paris Military Library, who had previously written to Grierson that his *Pensées et Essais* contained things "so exact and so profound."[10] Paul Bourget was yet another writer whose company in the secluded Faubourg Saint-Germain section of Paris Grierson cherished. His closest association among French writers was with René François Sully-Prud-homme who had followed the progress of Grierson's career since the days in 1869 when he had heard the young musician play at the salon of the Marquise de Ricard.

One of Grierson's few poetic efforts was a privately printed, seventy-five line poem called "A Grecian Rhapsody" which he dedicated to Sully-Prudhomme.[11] Inconsequential as poetry, it nevertheless indicates Grierson's longing for a far-off romanticism, in many ways as difficult to pinpoint and describe as his mysticism. The setting for the poem is Mt. Parnassus where the Muses are found engaged in revelry with nymphs, satyrs, and fauns. Moonlight washes the scene with an effulgence of mystical whiteness. With the coming of dawn, which Grierson ironically calls the "sunrise of new worlds," the group vanishes. Gone is its "Lydian music" and gone too, Grierson infers, are the Romantic poets of a past day who found their inspiration at Mt. Parnassus. What prevails instead, Grierson continued, is some kind of Nietzschean madness or, even worse, the cold sterility of science. Unsettling to Grierson was his sense of alienation with the current philosophic presupposition which showed man, on the one hand, to be only a mechanical object and, on the other, a thoroughly irrational, unpredictable victim of instinct. The times were badly out of joint with his own disposition. But, as is evident in this poem to Sully-Prudhomme, he would try to overcome the unpleasantness of "new worlds" by fashioning a dreamy and romantic mysticism of his own.

In this poem is the vagueness and dim melancholy that Edgar Allan Poe wrote about in his "The Philosophy of Composition." Convinced that poetry should suggest these distant regions of romantic wonder, Grierson created a tonal language which he thought poetically parallel to the musical effects he wove with the piano. In this poem is an almost complete absence of sharpness, realistic detail, and intellectual imagery. Its key is its resemblance to music, which Grierson came to regard as the most sublime of all art. Its subject matter disappears in a misty romanticism, and what remains is itself the melancholy evidence that Grierson's poetry was only some last outcroppings of a dying Romantic mode.

As mentioned earlier, Grierson's literary output before 1899 was meager. He still attended to his music, traveling to most of the important European courts where he gave recitals. In 1892 he visited the Duke and Duchess of Cumberland at their palace in Gmunden, Austria. For this occasion he had expected only the members of the Cumberland family, but Princess Thyra of Denmark, who was the Duchess of Cumberland, had invited both her mother, who was the Queen of Hanover, and the reigning Duke of Saxe-Altenburg. For this illustrious group and, as Tonner described the scene, amid an "indescribable medieval glamour ... created by the wax tapers, the dark, carved woods, the stags' horns, and the romantic ensemble,"[12] Grierson improvised his haunting music. At the end of the evening he quietly disappeared with Tonner.

While the exact dates are difficult if not impossible to set, Grierson gave recitals in homes, for societies, and at courts in Munich, Berlin, Hamburg, Leipzig, Dresden, Stuttgart, and

Karlsruhe. In Dresden he dedicated the Strelitz Palace music room of the Queen of Saxony, an elaborate occasion at which King Albert, the queen, and all the royal family were present. For this performance Grierson received a ruby ring surrounded with diamonds which he wore from that time on. Further travel took him in 1895 to London where, except for a brief tour later to the Continent, he stayed for the next eighteen years. He continued to play before small audiences, but his main interest was now in writing.

A short time before *Modern Mysticism* was published, Grierson thought of changing his name. He was now more serious about his literary career than he had been in San Diego, and he wanted to assure himself that no earlier reputation he had made as a musician, free-lancer, and California Spiritualist would endanger his incipient one as a literary essayist. Consequently, he took the name of Francis Grierson, and *Modern Mysticism* appeared in 1899 as his initial literary work. For how long the secret of his former identity was kept is uncertain. Maurice Maeterlinck, for one, assured Tonner by letter that he would never reveal Grierson's earlier name. But Grierson himself soon strategically realized that his biography, if made public, would add luster to his new name. He therefore wrote a short account of himself to introduce his next book, *The Celtic Temperament;* approximately two thousand words long, this introduction gives the fullest story about himself that he ever published.

Modern Mysticism, a thin volume of short essays, treats such subjects as art, beauty, nature, and wisdom—favorite subjects for late nineteenth-century Romantics clinging, as they were, to the dying hopes of a lingering era. Grierson's essays are delicately woven into a single theme—"modern mysticism"—by which he believed modern man could yet recover his lost sense of wonder and divine imaginings. Grierson's emphasis upon "modern" highlighted, by contrast, what he thought were the ponderous "medieval" dogmas of the church which, Grierson thought, fettered the spirit and thereby nullified mysticism. In its way, *Modern Mysticism* is a remarkable little book. In reading it one thinks of what Nathaniel Hawthorne said about his own *Twice-Told Tales*: that his stories would fade and be lost if exposed too long to the sunshine. Grierson's essays in this book, to extend the metaphor, are like slender goblets which sparkle exquisitely when left alone in recessed light.

Reviewers were favorably impressed by the book, written as it was for a discriminating audience. *The Spectator* commended Grierson for the way he managed "the most difficult of literary forms, the essay."[13] *The Westminster Review* first noted his "rare intuition and a profound knowledge both of art and human nature" and then applauded the entire work: "Many of the aphorisms in the volume are not only most original, but also most penetrative from the standpoint of the artist and the student.... The little volume is indeed a treasure-house of thought and critical acumen."[14] Other reviewers both in England and Scotland thought the book uncommonly provocative.

Many friends re-echoed these same sentiments. Maurice Maeterlinck, for example, said that Grierson had succeeded in "curiously and admirably" showing life with its "grand and simple profundities, humane and general conscience, and [had seen] an infinite and most touching vast truth."[15] Another note came from Fiona Macleod, the fictional Scottish woman whom William Sharp, one of the Celtic Renaissance leaders, referred to as his cousin, but who was Sharp himself under a pseudonym. After reading the book, "Fiona Macleod" wrote that "Mr. Sharp, my kinsman as well as my friend," had told her how the book had "immediately and profoundly" impressed him. "She" agreed that "it is a book with much in it to ponder—the kind of book I love."[16]

With the 1901 publication of *The Celtic Temperament* Grierson's theme shifted to more immediate situations, for he saw in contemporary England the oncoming end of philosophic idealism and, with it, social aristocracy. He saw these vast traditions giving way to rationalism, positivism, and scientism, including Darwinism which, to him, meant a denial of fixed species, an attack upon Christian morality, and a dehumanized scientific method. What he found in the term *fin-de-siècle* was more than a point of time. To him a civilization was losing its capacity to absorb the mysteries of the supernatural. He looked back to the old Celts whose temperament, he thought, most ideally coalesced with the world of spirit. This Celtic temperament was absent in the modern age.

Again Grierson received notable critical attention. William James told him he found the book "charming, and full of wisdom."[17] He especially thought the essay "Hebraic Inspiration" striking. In it Grierson had decried the "inharmony" and the "stubborness" of current philosophical disputes. Six years later James would publish *Pragmatism* in an effort to mediate the specific dispute between the extremes of idealism and Spencerian naturalism. Sharing Grierson's impatience with philosophical hagglers, James agreed that such discussions too often end in personal vanity, ambition, and strife. What James found impressive in Grierson's essay was his advice to the "hair-splitting" philosophers to seek the wisdom spoken by the Hebrew prophets. This was the wisdom, according to Grierson, which affirmed that through religious experiences a person can attain superhuman consciousness.

It is significant that in neither Grierson's essay nor in James's reply was anything said about the God under whose power these prophets lived. The fact is that Grierson rarely mentioned God in anything he wrote, and he never discussed in his essays such Christian convictions as sin, grace, and atonement. To Grierson, God was a supreme mind, an all-seeing power, an invisible force; in the essay on "Hebraic Inspiration" he used such terms as "one spirit," "one impulsion," "one source and aim animating the whole." This is hardly the Hebrew's God about whom Grierson said the prophets "all spoke with one voice," another less than accurate detail. Nor is Grierson's ideal man, whose wisdom of the divine comes from his own self-fulfillment, the religious person represented in Hebrew tradition. But attitudes such as these failed to disturb James or other persons who praised the book.

Austin Harrison of the *English Review* thought *The Celtic Temperament* a "delightful book.[18] Robert H. Davis, associate editor of *Munsey's Magazine* in New York, wrote to Grierson that the book was "a storehouse of brilliant analysis and subtle understanding set forth in a style so fascinating that it cannot be forgotten."[19] Benjamin De Casseres, the American writer, said, "I stood stock still in the library as I read. . . . You have the ability of saying a thing simply and tremendously."[20] The first critical notice to be published in an American periodical announced Grierson as "one of the cleverest of the present generation of English essayists. He has all the brilliancy of Mr. Chesterton without his eccentricities." The same reviewer predicted that "if Mr. Grierson goes on writing as clever essays . . . he will be sure to receive the recognition that such writing compels sooner or later."[21]

But Grierson's momentum did not last. Just when his work had begun to attract fairly wide notice, his output sharply declined. In the next five years he published only eight essays, five of which appeared again in later books. The reason for Grierson's withdrawal remains one more of Grierson's enigmas. The question is whether he put everything aside to write *The Valley of Shadow*, his next work which appeared eight years later. In a cryptic note he declared that it "took me ten years to write [*The Valley of Shadows*], and all my fortune to the *last* silver shilling. When the last page was finished the last shilling was spent."[22] One thing is certain: his extended period of silence hurt his literary reputation. Edwin Björkman correctly summarized that, "had he continued without interruption to produce books of the same kind, his reputation might have spread more rapidly among the public at large."[23]

During these years preceding the publication of *The Valley of Shadows*, Grierson austerely withdrew from public life. Van Wyck Brooks, who saw him occasionally in London during this time, wrote that Grierson was "solitary, poor and all but forgotten."[24] In his *Scenes and Portraits* (1954) Brooks offered a much longer account:

How many strange fish, for the rest, one found inhabiting the depths of the ocean of London, living in clefts of the rocks, seldom visiting the surface. One was the old essayist Francis Grierson about whom I had heard so much,—Edwin Björkman had written a paper on him. He was said to live over a grocer's shop somewhere in Twickenham, although no one saw him there or knew his address; but he would emerge in response to a letter at the Bridge House in Richmond, where he received admirers and correspondents. There meetings were promptly written up in the local newspaper, the *Twickenham Times,* the readers of which were led to suppose that Grierson was a literary potentate to whom all the great of the earth made pilgrimages. For, humble as the guest might be, he was described as a world-famous professor or some other sort of lion or cock of the walk, the secret of it being that Grierson had a Sancho Panza who not only served as a press-agent but supported him as well. He worked for a small wage, I think, as a tailor's assistant. When Grierson dined with my wife and me and I took him to the door to say good-night, there was a strange man sitting on the steps,—it was Waldemar Tonner, the Polish-American whom Grierson announced as his secretary and who had been waiting there all the evening through.

Continuing in the same account, Brooks then described the physical appearance of this pathetically humorous "fish."

> There was a touch of the charlatan in him, but there was a curious innocence too in this tall man with his worn old tweeds, his drooping moustache, pink cheeks, and crimson necktie. The moustache was evidently dyed and he rouged his cheeks, and that he wore a wig was also apparent from the white hairs that straggled out over his ears; and later when he was caught by the rain and obliged to stay in my house I was sorry that I could not help him in the matter of cosmetics. How without rouge would he be able to appear in the morning, not so speak of wax for his moustache. But only his wig was askew when he came down blithely.[25]

No doubt Brooks enjoyed writing this sketch of Grierson who cut a strange figure indeed, but Brooks was delicate enough to leave open the subject of Grierson's extra-literary association with Tonner. The important fact about Grierson at this time is his ambition to publish a really first-rate book. His absence from social hobnobbing and his apparently self-imposed isolation (Mary Austin reported that all this time he was "living with books"[26]) suggest he was following an idea, dear to Romantics, that creativity requires withdrawal from the world. The outcome of these years was *The Valley of Shadows*.

To write it, he went back to the years when he lived in the Middle West amid the exciting times of camp-meetings, the Underground Railway, and the last of the Lincoln-Douglas debates. He recalled the prophecies of the frontiersmen, the anxieties of all who knew a civil war was inevitable, and the role of the Emancipator as it was conceived by rural seers. And so, after having spent many years away from the prairies, Grierson imaginatively returned to them. For a person accustomed to urban and court amenities, Grierson's success in portraying pioneer life was the more remarkable. *The Valley of Shadows* shaped the deep impressions of his childhood. With this book he brought them to the surface at a time when his idealism demanded a narrative. His recollection of the mysticism of the Middle West served this purpose. The importance of the book warrants a close analysis in a later chapter.

Grierson greatly accelerated his literary work after *The Valley of Shadows* was published. Early in 1909 he signed a contract with James Allen, financial supporter for *The New Age*, a peri-

odical which at this time published work of H. G. Wells, George
Bernard Shaw, G. K. Chesterton, Hilaire Belloc, and Arnold
Bennett. From January 28, 1909, to January 11, 1911, Grierson
submitted a total of forty-nine essays, many of which re-appeared
without change in his three books *Parisian Portraits* (1911), *The
Humour of the Underman* (1911), and *The Invincible Alliance*
(1913). Again publicly active, he also wrote for *The Nation* and
for *The English Review.*

Grierson felt rejuvenated after he had finished his long-labored
chef d'oeuvre. With arrangements made to continue sending
essays to *The New Age,* he left for Italy in the spring of 1910, his
first departure from England in fifteen years. Unfortunately, his
short stay in Florence depressed him. The country seemed "worn
out," its languor settling over everything. And touring the
Continent again only reinforced his certainty that, for all its aim-
lessness, modern Europe was heading toward a gigantic war.

Grierson's gloomy disposition in Italy disturbed Arnold Bennett
with whom he dined in Florence. Bennett, at forty-five, had completed *The Old Wives' Tale* two years earlier and was now, in
1910, awaiting the publication of his second great success,
Clayhanger. Fascinated by vast enterprises and by the prospects
of wealth, Bennett was annoyed with Grierson who, said Bennett,
"was evidently poor" and yet unaccountably aloof about money
matters. According to Bennett's account in his appropriately entitled *The Savour of Life: Essays in Gusto* (1928), Grierson
resembled

> those grumbling, girding painters, musicians, writers, and dilet-
> tanti—quite a large class—who have far less brains than he [Grier-
> son] had, and whose reasoning about money, if their mental
> processes can be called reasoning, is fatally affected by cerebral
> sloth, general incapacity, and a revolting artistic snobbishness.
>
> These parasites on society cannot, or apparently will not,
> understand that the first duty of, for instance, a poet is not to
> write poetry, but to keep himself in decency, and his wife and
> children if he has them, to discharge his current obligations, and
> to provide for old age. . . .[27]

As a Realist who wrote of the unromantic commonplaces, Bennett found Grierson an exceedingly enigmatic person. After
dining with him in England, Bennett wrote in his *Journals* that
"Grierson made a peculiar effect on me."[28] When he saw him
two years later in Italy, Grierson still impressed Bennett as a

"mysterious person."[29] Slightly fidgety, Bennett was intrigued by this elderly gentleman whose wig was so curiously long and whose moustache was always dyed. Grierson, who would not dress for dinner; who ate most of his meals in his hotel room; who, when asked by Bennett if he was paid for his articles in *The New Age*, obscurely replied no, saying only that " 'somebody else pays me' " and hinting that he had lost his money—Grierson, an incongruous and anachronistic Romantic, puzzled Bennett who was a vigorous and practical man. Bennett recognized Grierson as "a sensitive and highly cultivated man" who had "taste" and who knew "a great deal about the arts, politics, and the way the human mind works." But he could not overlook the fact that Grierson's popularity was not so widespread as his own. Though intrigued, Bennett finally dismissed Grierson as a writer who had a considerable reputation among only a few people. Furthermore, not impressed by Grierson's success as a piano improvisator, he put him aside as "second-rate."[30]

The two allegations coming from Bennett were that Grierson (1) had a limited literary reputation, and (2) was only a second-rate musician. To a certain degree this appraisal is correct. Yet it does hide something remarkable about Grierson's last years in England. When Grierson returned in the summer to his Twickenham address, he arranged for the immediate publication of *Parisian Portraits*. During the next year two more books were published, *The Humour of the Underman* and *La Vie et les Hommes*. Before returning to the United States in 1913, he published *The Invincible Alliance*. To what extent did these works increase his reputation during these final years? Furthermore, what were people saying about his musicianship?

Before answering the first question, we may look briefly at the contents of these four books. In *Parisian Portraits* he gathered his best essays about persons whom he had known in Paris. Though too eager to hail them all with equal favor, he wrote with considerable precision and fluency about Verlaine, Sully-Prudhomme, Mallarmé, Lamartine, and Leconte de Lisle. He had spoken personally to each of these men, except Alphonse Lamartine; and he considered them all to be giants in French literature during the Second Empire and the Third Republic. *The Humour of the Underman* is Grierson's most important volume dealing with art and esthetics. His essays on "Art, Science, and Beauty," "The Classical and the Critical," "Feeling and Intellect,"

and "The Humour of the Underman" (seen in Uncle Remus' art-
less yet supremely instinctive expression) unfold his central
ideas about proportion, simplicity, and the universality of art—as
well as those about artistic feeling, intuition, catholicity, and
spontaneity. His third book of this period, *La Vie et les Hommes*,
contains collected aphorisms on artistic and philosophic subjects
treated far more substantially in other works.

In his last published work in England, *The Invincible Alliance*,
he set forth his social and political theories. Underlying the essays
in this book is an incipient hysteria about the German menace
in Europe and about the Yellow menace in Asia. He believed
that the only hope for controlling these "juggernauts of materialism and primitivism" was an alliance among all English-speaking
peoples. If, as he wrote in the essay "The New Era," this alliance
could hold, then "a new era will bring with it a spiritual renaissance and the unity of the Anglo-American people" (235).

What then of Bennett's claim that Grierson's literary reputation
existed only among a few people? Sales warranted a second edition of *Parisian Portraits* in 1911, of *The Celtic Temperament* in
1911, and of *The Humour of the Underman* in 1913. *The Valley
of Shadows* appeared in a third edition when Grierson sailed
from England in 1913. Moreover, each of these books was favorably reviewed in scores of English, Scottish, and American
periodicals, the latter frequently claiming Grierson as a native
son. In 1912, *Current Literature* reported in a lengthy article that
"in this country an interest in Grierson is spreading widely." The
Boston *Athenaeum* hailed his style "a compliment to the intelligence of his audience." The New York *Times* noted his role as
"a constructive cynic," and the *Dial* praised his "unique rapier
and sabre attack." To the Boston *Transcript* reviewer, Grierson's
mind showed a "clearness of insight ... understanding of conditions ... absolute seriousness and earnestness ... sincerity of
vision."[31]

Bennett's other assertion concerning Grierson as a "second-
rate" musician is difficult to evaluate, for none of his improvisations was ever preserved in writing. Grierson thought that to
keep such music nullified the rationale of the art itself. While
such practice raises weighty psychological problems in understanding Grierson's kind of Romanticism, it is clear that he
identified himself with a musical tradition dignified by Paganini,
Schumann, and Brahms, and, during Grierson's days in France,

by Liszt. It was a tradition uniquely suited to Grierson who, once he discovered and then developed his musical skills, went on to realize in improvisation a way to express his deeply mystical feelings. He sensed in creation a vital force too deep for words but nevertheless open to the power of music. In whatever theme he chose to develop, he thought its intrinsic spirituality could be intimated through music.

Proof of Grierson's musical power must come from the testimony of listeners, tenuous as this evidence is. During his last years in London listeners repeatedly said that Grierson, whose hands stretched to an octave and a half, produced weird and emotionally powerful music. Some of it evoked the characteristics of past musical epochs. Other times it re-created the musical soul of ancient Egypt, Assyria, Palestine, and Greece. One evening John Lane, the English publisher, heard Grierson play, and his reaction was typical. Grierson had been improvising on and on; the twilight had been deepening. Finally, in the gloom he improvised on the sinking of the *Titanic*. Lane said that Grierson's treatment was so overwhelming that it moved him to postpone for a fortnight his departure for America, although he had arranged to sail the very next day.[32]

Word of Grierson's performances preceded his own arrival in the United States. When he landed in New York he was acclaimed not only as a "musical liberator" but also as "the most authentic and far-seeing personality of our time."[33] In a widely read review Edwin Björkman described one of Grierson's home concerts:

It opened with a procession of chords—haunting, monotonous, primitive. It was as if the horns and drums of some African village had become civilized without losing their original weirdness—as if their uncouth noises had become miraculously transformed into genuine harmonies while still echoing the strife of primeval passions. Something more than sound issued from that piano: it was a mood "uncanny," yet pleasing, exalting, luring.

He seemed to keep notes suspended in the air for minutes. Now and then he would make a shining vessel out of such a chord, and then he would begin to drip little drops of melody into it, until the Grail seemed to rise before your vision, luminous with blood-red rubies....

"This is an ancient Egyptian improvisation—" Apparently Mr. Grierson had spoken, and his words were passed around in whispers. Again a complete change of atmosphere followed. The form of the previous pieces had been comparatively vague; now the design of the composition was sharply outlined—and as it revealed itself, the perfection of that design became increasingly evident. The music was quaint, but not Oriental in any accepted sense. Its opening passages were characterized by harmonies that I can only describe as "brittle," and that suggested the violin rather than the piano. Then the music swelled and became strangely urgent—I felt there was an image that wanted to break through—a consciousness of some mighty presence—and all at once it was there: "The Nile!"[34]

Grierson's arrival in the United States marked the end of his major writing. His achievement both in music and in literature had been remarkable up to that time, and his reputation was more substantial than Arnold Bennett asserted. It is to Grierson's major phase as a writer—to the ideas in the seven books written during this period, from 1889 to 1913—that we now turn.

CHAPTER 4

Social Views

I *End of an Era*

G RIERSON ARRIVED in France during the turbulent last days of the Second Empire. The victorious armies of Bismarck and von Moltke soon ended an era that had been recklessly bent on pleasure, pageantry, and extravagance. It is true that the Empire had virtually won back for France its cultural leadership and had modernized Paris. Its pleasure-loving emperor, Charles Louis Napoleon Bonaparte, third son of the king of Holland, and its dazzling Empress Eugénie de Montijo, formerly a Spanish countess, had set a pace for Parisian high life which inspired those on the lower rungs of the social ladder to follow. Even the vast working population, before its awakening to the Franco-Prussian War, had let itself be lulled by its own penny pleasures. But the debacle at Sedan in 1870 ended this era. The scepticism and fatalism of Taine, the Goncourt brothers, Zola, and Baudelaire mirrored a new era of disenchantment.

Grierson, who was present at the finale of the Second Empire, wrote in *Parisian Portraits* that it was a time when "people were passing out of the world of romance and had not yet arrived at that of realism" (10). He interpreted 1870 as a year of finality in France, for the curtain had dropped on a play whose theme, despite its frivolity, had been one of social peace and well-being. When a similar curtain came down in England in 1901, perhaps more slowly but just as decisively, Grierson was again present; on that cheerless January day of a new century he watched Queen Victoria's cortege pass through the London streets. Because Grierson was apprehensive about the show to follow, he spent much of his life in the old theater, after the drama was over, amid the lingering smells of stale smoke and wilted chrysanthemums.

II *Between Two Worlds*

Grierson criticized the social excesses—the dandyism and smugness—he had witnessed in Paris before 1870 with no less vigor than he rebuked English manners during the decades before and after the end of the century. Yet in his attitude toward the France of Napoleon III he ambivalently delighted in the same elegant excesses which he attempted to appraise critically. He never lost his fascination for the courts, salons, and the theaters which, like bright jewels, continued to sparkle in his memory. He treasured souvenirs from the nobility, boasted of his acquaintances, furnished Villa Montezuma as a show place with their gifts, and in his last days valued above all else his ruby ring which, two weeks before his death, he pathetically pawned for bread money. This ambivalence of position is merely another facet of the same quality which marked his entire life. It is not surprising, therefore, that his criticism of the Empire's giddiness before 1870 comes short of explaining his own fascination with it.

The drama in France whose epilogue Grierson observed began in 1848 with a tempestuous but short introduction. The revolution lasted only four months, the bourgeoisie taking over again with Louis-Napoleon Bonaparte (Napoleon II) as emperor. By 1852 the pomp and ceremony easily exceeded that of Louis Philippe's court. The military became a highly privileged class, its armies supposedly invincible. Anatole France described Paris under Napoleon II as "l'auberge du monde."[1] Night after night Hortense Schneider gaily sang Jacques Offenbach's music. At the Exposition of 1867, which Grierson later described as "the beginning of the end of the Third Napoleon's fabulous and romantic reign,"[2] her stage dressing room was so packed with noblemen and foreigners that it was named the Passage of Princes. The fashionable tastes found expression in Offenbach who strutted forth in yellow trousers and waistcoat, grey gloves, coat of sky-blue, a green hat, the whole outfit topped by a red umbrella. All this gaiety Grierson interpreted later as a sign that Paris in 1869 was drugged, the court deliriously happy, and the entire nation blind to the idea of sedition and war. People ate, drank, and were merry; in the evening they crowded theaters, operas, and cafés. He wrote in *Parisian Portraits* that it was a time when nobles and the bourgeoisie enjoyed Offenbach's "inane" melodies as they sat in their cushioned seats and waited, "like fatted oxen in their stalls, the butchery of the morrow" (25).

Underlying this description is Grierson's more significant complaint, not so much against these follies as against those which followed in the Third Republic. He granted that ostentation had marred the Second Empire, but he far more bitterly asserted that vulgarity came after. What he called the "wonderful, romantic movement" in *Parisian Portraits,* he saw transformed by the "reign of the commonplace." Sadly he watched "the lions of romance" depart—Hugo, Lamartine, and George Sand. In their place came "the jackals of realism" including Zola who "had already begun to gnaw the bones left by Balzac." Never was Grierson more expressive of outrage than in *Parisian Portraits* when he called these literary jackals "a school of hydrocephalic and colour-blinded artists" (10, 145).

His unrest, indeed his rage, grew from the relentless truth that the aristocratic, the traditional, and the conservative no longer ruled society. To his distress a new middle class and an ever-growing laboring class were arrogating the men and women of fashion, idlers for the most part, refined and aristocratic. It was among this latter group that Grierson found his element. The world of Zola held terror for him. The coal miners in Zola's *Germinal* (1885); the peasants in *La Terre* (1887); Coupeau, Gervaise, and Nana amid squalor and sexual immorality in *L'Assommoir* (1887)—these were subjects Grierson sharply turned away from. He saw himself as a genteel, cultivated artist whose world was generically different from that which Zola depicted.

It should be remembered that, even though French Realists were raking muck heaps for subject matter, they were also as frequently inclined toward the *haute monde* as was Grierson. Erich Auerbach points out, for example, that Gustave Flaubert and the Goncourts were comfortably housed; they ate exquisitely and indulged every craving of their refined taste. For the well-born Edmond and Jules de Goncourt the slum population had something of the same exoticism which the salon had for Grierson. Even as pre-eminent Realists they sought the exotic in the ugly and claimed the two could be reconciled within the world of art.[3] Grierson's presuppositions rigidly distinguished between subjects as either inherently poetic or not. To associate literature with the ugly destroyed for Grierson the *raison d'être* of art. He could never recognize, for example, an esthetic force behind the

Goncourts' *Germanie Lacerteux* (1864), a novel describing the sexual entanglement and gradual ruin of a housemaid. On the other hand, he insisted that despite its extravagance there remained something esthetically authentic about aristocratic society and what he considered its romantic art.

It is evident that Grierson did not intend *Parisian Portraits* to do more than gently remind the socially élite of its occasional excesses. Grierson certainly saw no indication of social decay and impending doom when, for example, Princess Bonaparte-Rattazzi said to him: " 'Cette soirée est pour vous, vous savez,' " and then ushered him and her other guests to a table set with forty gold plates upon which were engraved the imperial arms. Instead, her apartment with its "series of blue boudoirs" seemed to Grierson to be "suspended between the heavens and the earth as a fairyland... a living picture from Monte Cristo or the Arabian Nights" (30-32). He saw nothing but rare elegance, a place set apart especially for poets and artists whose sensibilities, to Grierson, required this kind of atmosphere. To him, the quintessence of civilized society was to be found in a French salon—one like Dumas' with its mystery and romantic atmosphere, or like the Marquise de Ricard's with its "soft colours, its long, heavy curtains, and its thick *tapis de moquette*."[4] These salons represented the world of refinement and leisure, allowing for none of the bourgeois energies common to business and social climbing. In Jamesian terms the salons were dense, rich, and warm. They were places of enchantments, enchanters, and, above all, enchantresses.

When Grierson had his own salon, the Villa Montezuma in San Diego, he knew exactly how to indulge his taste. Reminiscent of the Hotel Pimodan where the bohemians Gautier and Baudelaire first met in 1849, Grierson's Villa exuded the same kind of mysterious exoticism. His clever departure from San Diego did not lessen his desire for the gem-like flame which illumined these dazzling and always semi-secluded sanctuaries. During his long residence in England he found distressingly little to compare with the French salons or with his own Villa Montezuma. As one historian has said, during the Edwardian period "one might have searched in vain in fashionable London for anything fit to be called a *salon*."[5] Yet certainly one of the most curious facts about Grierson is that he had nothing to do with the conspicuous English literary figures of the decade who maintained exotic suites and whose tastes so closely paralleled his own. He never belonged to their Rhymers' Club. He had no association with Aubrey Beardsley or Henry Harland, and he contributed nothing either to their quarterly, *The Yellow Book,* or to Arthur Symons' *The Savoy.* He thought Swinburne a master of style but paid no attention to Oscar Wilde. Only in his association with John Lane did Grierson touch the English literary movement of estheticism. As publisher of *The Yellow Book,* Lane continually fished London for new talent, found Grierson, and published four of his books.

The reason Grierson kept apart from the celebrated English contemporaries whose tastes matched his own was his differing viewpoint toward the writer's responsibilities. He did not agree to a principle which held the artist responsible only to art. What he saw among the English esthetes was indifference to religion, morality, education, politics, and society. Their credo of "art for art's sake" had come from Théophile Gautier who had asserted that "moral purpose, deep thought, sage and prudent reflection, all worn and respectable trappings of the creative spirit were irrelevant to its free expression."[6] This aloofness from social issues Grierson found inimical to his own sustained observation of them. Had Grierson, even as a minor figure, joined the company of esthetes, he might not have been a strange fish lost in London's shadowy recesses. But, instead of joining forces with the esthetic movement of the 1890's, he exiled himself in the backwaters; there he held to moral and critical principles generally repudiated by his more well-known contemporaries. Yet he chose, at least some of the time, to play the role of social critic, to leave his world of strange music and reminiscences in order to look out onto the streets, and to see there the swirling bits of chaff representing for him English middle-class society.

III Attack upon Middle Class

Grierson's displeasure with the English middle class was first expressed in his account of its complacency toward the French defeat of 1870. One of the first subjects he took up when he began writing in 1887 was the ominous significance of this debacle. During the years which followed, he kept his eye on the growing manufacturing and military strength of Germany, so that by the time he wrote *The Invincible Alliance* in 1913, his fears were implacable: "if the Prussian in 1870 was a fighting

automaton with a will wound up like a clock, what would he be
now after forty years of drill, and discipline far more reasoned,
far more desperate" (19). What Grierson found both unaccountable and inexcusable was England's lack of concern about what
he regarded as a growing German menace. In looking back over
the years since 1870, he said he remembered seeing in London
and the great manufacturing centers only so many people content
to live on year after year in a state of "chronic apathy" and
"mock security" (22).

It is relevant to note that Grierson's account of British complacency resembles that of G. M. Trevelyan who said that, though
the Franco-Prussian war in 1870 made his countrymen vaguely
aware that something was going on among "those unaccountable
foreigners," the English were too absorbed in their own business
to bother about Continental defeat and revolution.[7] If the general
public showed any interest in the French catastrophe, he said, it
was merely to point out that the nation's defeat was a just punishment for her sins and decadence, an explanation which R. J.
Cruikshank shows to be almost identical to the one the English
used to account for France's collapse in 1940.[8] George Meredith's
theme in the poem "France: 1870" was the same: the French
defeat vindicated the moral order. The English could not resist
contrasting the tinsel of the Tuileries with the solid mahogany
virtues of Parliament, and they also tended to distrust French
Catholics and atheists more than German Protestants. The
French, after all, were frivolous creatures far outdistanced in
the competitive race of Progress. With gentle condescension, the
English looked on the Continent as a different and inferior world.

To generalize about a nation's temperament is always risky.
Exceptions abound if the single label "complacency," as used by
Grierson, serves to describe the English during the three decades
following 1870. A wave of pessimism did sweep across the
Channel from defeated France and sent many men of letters to
find consolation in the world of art. Furthermore, England's
agricultural problems by 1875 were becoming acute. The decline
of wheat acreage, followed by similar reduction of farm laborers
and prices, led to agricultural depressions over much of England
and Wales. At the same time, the persistent feeling that all was
not well with the social system, especially in larger industrial
cities, agitated many English intellectuals, including novelists.
Nevertheless, at the risk of oversimplification, it can be said that

the last thirty years of Queen Victoria's reign were prosperous. The Queen's Jubilee of 1887 and especially her Diamond Jubilee of 1897 drew attention to a vast, powerful, and wealthy realm. The pageantry of the Empire, the confidence of Kipling's verse, the winning back of the Sudan in 1898 from the French at the battle of Omdurman—all these, despite the shadows creeping into the picture, provided ample reason for nearly any aging Victorian to say, "John Bull feels sure of himself."

It was the imperturbably complacent Englishman whom Grierson scorned, especially the parvenu who never questioned the implications of *laissez-faire,* who saw nothing but progress ahead, whose faith in industry was unshakable, whose highest value was material well-being, and whose measurement of success was always tied with wealth. At this person Grierson aimed vituperative criticism. It must be made clear that Grierson was not preaching a social gospel. He did not argue about the socio-economic philosophies of Claude St. Simon and François Fourier in France, or of Adam Smith, John Ruskin, William Morris, or Karl Marx in England. Neither did he get involved with the novelists who were asking important social questions about labor and urbanization. Instead, he studied what an old-fashioned Victorian would call the moral dry rot of a society epitomized no longer by *noblesse oblige* but rather by the new motto, "money talks."

Among this increasingly wealthy and powerful bourgeoisie, which by the time of Edward's reign Grierson said lacked even the dignity to imitate aristocratic manners, Matthew Arnold found his now-famous "philistines." In joining Arnold's protest, Grierson used the terms "vulgar" and "blindly ambitious" to describe this same group. He noticed how the well-oiled efficiency of modern finance enabled a person to turn so much wealth into its equivalent in luxury without any requisite of culture. He observed the parvenu posing as a patron of art, though all the while refusing to give the artists the same freedom of expression implicit in the businessman's license of *laissez-faire*. And he scorned the philistine's shallow optimism and sentimental religiosity, qualities more repellent to him than intransigent pessimism and agnosticism.

In his essay "The Social Half-Way House" in *The Humour of the Underman,* Grierson described the social climber, one who because of wealth has come "half-way" but who will go no farther because of cultural vacuity. This particular climber, a woman in Grierson's essay, has an air of "feigned assurance," the required "grace of manner," "little tricks of speech," an "affectation of sympathy and appreciation" necessary to get on. She is a member of the "smart set," plutocrats and parasites.

> She is a person who lacks some power or combination of talents, to attain a place on or near the social summit. She conforms to social routine; is, of course, lacking in originality; seldom makes an independent move, for fear of being compromised. . . . For the mistress has long since abandoned the idea of going against the tide, of taking absurd risks. . . . The house exists, not so much from lack of means to dare and to do, as from lack of moral courage to be simple and sincere (32-33).

Grierson's charges against the English middle class are echoed in his social views of American life. Even though he did his major writing in England, he distastefully remembered the American profiteers during the Civil War, their unconcern for the national cause and their disgusting conspicuousness. During the short time he and his family lived at Niagara Falls, young Grierson saw vacationers aplenty: women chiefly concerned with the costliness of their dresses and the "lucky" industrialists whom the war was making wealthy. He also remembered seeing as a youth the crowds of Chicago women leaving a summer matinee performance, "arrayed in garments that would have petrified the Queen of Sheba with envy." This and other statements about American society Grierson put into an essay he entitled "The Doom of American Democracy," written in England at the beginning of his major literary period. The "doom" was the growing social influence enjoyed by Northern industrial families whose conspicuous and tasteless splendors "were the special gifts" from the God of War.[9]

Grierson was part of the widespread literary hostility against the growing middle class. Scores of novels depicted the intrusion of pretenders into the traditional upper classes. Hjalmar Boyesen mercilessly exposed the social climber in *Mammon of Unrighteousness* (1891) and in *The Social Strugglers* (1893). Edith Wharton's *House of Mirth* (1905) described the slow corruption of New York aristocracy by the aggressive entrepreneurs. Earlier treatments were of course Mark Twain's *The Gilded Age* (1873) and William Dean Howells' *The Rise of Silas Lapham* (1885).

Merle Curti has said that by the end of the nineteenth century more than sixty novels had been written about what H. L. Mencken called *boobus americanus*.[10] Later critics including Van Wyck Brooks, Matthew Josephson, and V. F. Calverton asserted that the Gilded Age, with all its boorish upstarts, had impaled the creative artist who was unfortunate enough to remain in the United States.

Such present-day historians as Professors Curti, Henry Steele Commager, and Henry F. May, who have described the influence of the *nouveau riche* upon post-Civil War culture, take their cue from another historian who spoke out in attributing the decay of artistic imagination to an economic intellect and a materialistic culture. It was Brooks Adams who declared in the last chapter of his sensational *Law of Civilization and Decay* (1896):

> This mercenary quality forms the gulf which has divided the art of the Middle Ages from that of modern times—a gulf which cannot be bridged, and which has broadened with the lapse of centuries, until at last the artist, like all else in society, has become the creature of a commercial market, even as the Greek was sold as a slave to the plutocrat of Rome.... No poetry can bloom in the arid modern soil, the drama has died, and the patrons of art are no longer even conscious of shame at profaning the most sacred of ideals.[11]

In England, coincident with Grierson's first arrival in Europe, Arnold's *Culture and Anarchy* (1896) recommended culture as "the great help" out of the nation's social "difficulties." These difficulties were the consequences of power in the hands of philistines. After reading Tocqueville's *Democracy in America,* Arnold was determined to prevent England from becoming another gilded America. Other English writers linked these same difficulties with the qualities of grossness associated with social forces that emasculated aristocracy. To Swinburne, bourgeois respectability was one such force which he attacked symbolically by placing, on one celebrated occasion, the emblems of respectability—silk hats hanging in neat order on pegs—on the floor of the cloakroom adjacent to the auditorium of the Arts Club, and then hopping from one hat to the next crushing them in turn.[12] Wells, Bennett, and Shaw turned down enormous fees by refusing to write advertisements for a London store, claiming the offer was a condescending smear by mercantilism upon their identity as artists. On his famous 1892 lecture tour of the United States,

Oscar Wilde attempted to carry the gospel of art to the philistines whose cultural ignorance he recognized when he heard of an American traveler, returned from Europe, who was prepared to sue the express agency for having broken the arms of his purchased replica of Venus de Milo.

After ridiculing the middle-class pretenders, the artists had but a short step to take into total exile where they could affirm their autonomy, reject didacticism, and refuse to subject art to any moral or social judgment. Thus William York Tindall states at the outset of his survey of modern British literature that "the artist's exile from middle-class society accounts in part for the character" of late nineteenth-century literature.[13]

Vacillating between one pole and the other, Grierson did not accept the doctrine of "art for art's sake" with its gospel of social irrelevance. Yet he insisted in *The Humour of the Underman* that the artist was justified in remaining aloof: "The true artist ... has to avoid the influences both of the masses and the classes," living in the world but not "being controlled or influenced by it" (193). Where then does he function? According to Grierson, the artist lives apart from both society and nature, at least to the extent of his not being controlled by either. Grierson argued not only that the artist must withstand social influences but that he not be controlled willy-nilly by invisible forces operating in nature. He said that the artist on his mountain top (in company with Byron) "sees and hears and feels with Nature ... [and] absorbs and fuses all the meanings and mysteries of the world" (193). Assuming the English esthetes were able to penetrate this mystical, not to say misty, language, they would have cheered Grierson's insistence that the artist be aloof, but they also would have smiled at his reasons. The idea of seeing and hearing and feeling with nature, they would have found especially amusing; their first duty in life, as Oscar Wilde declared, was to be as artificial as possible and to cultivate what Holbrook Jackson called a "decadent dandyism."[14]

The line is thinly drawn between Grierson and the contemporary bohemians, decadents, and esthetes. His taste for the exotic was as carefully cultivated, his contempt for the middle class as unmitigated. He dyed his moustache, rouged his cheeks, and wore a wig. Yet he retained sufficient Victorian conventionality to adjudge bohemianism as vaguely unhealthy and to agree with Arnold that high seriousness must underlie art.

VI *Specific Indictments and Basic Antipathies*

Returning to Grierson's outrage over English manners, one finds four specific indictments. First, according to Grierson, the English had the unique distinction of being both great sportsmen and "moral cowards." Though what he meant by moral cowardice is never quite clear, he held to the idea that culture dominated by an aristocratic élite would be free from the kind of cowardly ruthlessness he saw rampant in business. At any rate, he found little that was morally edifying in English sport. He asserted in *Modern Mysticism* that the importance given to athletics in England since the days of Elizabeth had only encouraged evermore brutal sports—"football, fox-hunting, prize fighting"—all requiring plenty of muscle and physical courage but no brains nor moral independence (72).

On this subject Dixon Wecter predicted that someday sport would find its wide-visioned philosopher who will show why a certain game—cricket in England, bull fighting in Spain, baseball or football in America—belongs to a nation's pastime. He suggested that someone ought to explore Thomas Jefferson's remark in a letter to Peter Carr: "games played with a ball stamp no character on the mind."[15] Grierson was not the person to make this exploration, but he was puzzled, like Jefferson, over the same contradiction which Mark Twain explored in his essay, "Purchasing Civic Virtue." Said Twain, "it is odd that physical courage should be so common in the world and moral courage so rare."

Grierson's second criticism attacked English vulgarity, as he saw it at the turn of the century. Nothing particularly unique attaches itself to this observation except what Grierson saw going on in English clubs and music halls. To these institutions of middle-class culture he gives heavy-handed treatment in his essays "Style and Personality" and "The Spirit of the Music Hall" in *The Celtic Temperament*. He saw the old social clubs being invaded by a new class of people whose only credentials consisted of money. Something here struck Grierson as absurdly vulgar, especially as he watched how the patrons paid their dues merely to enjoy a *tête à tête* or to be amused. He readily admitted that the club served as an asylum from the raucous market place, but still he regretted to see the club changed into some kind of "human abattoir," a democratic "crematorium" (49, 50).

In short, it was not a salon. He saw it only as a place for forced wit, peurile gossip, fashionable dinners, and afternoon teas.

For music halls he had nothing but contempt. Regarding himself as a musical purist, he failed to appreciate the fact that music halls were the answer to people ill-served with amusement. Music halls had won their independence from the legitimate theaters, which had sought through prosecutions to close them; and now their performers went by cab from one music hall to the next, night after night, repeating their exhausting routine and playing with carefree lunacy the parts in Edward Lear's *Book of Nonsense* or Lewis Carroll's *Alice in Wonderland.* Grierson could take none of this entertainment. He called it "frenzied frivolity" and interpreted it as the "lolling license of a sordid democracy" (106, 108).

Going yet a little deeper, Grierson dredged up a third complaint, one against English snobbery as he saw it in the middle class. In his essay "The Prophet Without Honour" in *The Invincible Alliance,* he imagined a situation in which rumors had informed some social gadabouts that Tolstoy, stripped of his title and wealth, had just arrived in England. Upon hearing this news, the ladies and gentlemen are overjoyed—until they also hear about his hapless condition. Then they lose interest at once. Says Lady Prim, "In my opinion, when he lost his title he lost everything." As Grierson continues the story, a condescending oaf intended to typify middle-class snobbery says that he will gladly offer the broken writer a room in his servant's quarters where he can mend boots and write without bothering or embarrassing anyone. His scheme is to have first rights on Tolstoy, so that, when the writer dies and is buried in the garden, he can charge each visitor a shilling to view the grave. "His drawing power is gone now," he says, "but his grave will draw later on." By this sketch, which contains strangely autobiographical overtones, Grierson juxtaposed the artist and the philistine or, more accurately, illustrated how a bourgeois society goes about annihilating the artist while maintaining a self-righteous, unruffled, but conniving snobbism.

Grierson's fourth criticism exposed what he called English "fogyism," or a thoroughly rigid adherence to tradition. Himself a traditionalist, Grierson did not so much disclaim the value of tradition as rebuke the English for their inertia, their downright and adamant unwillingness to question the values they lived by.

To illustrate his point, Grierson cited perfunctory church attendance and the kind of English colonialism which resulted in cultural insularity. These conditions were symptomatic of what Grierson thought was fundamentally sick about English society. He saw that traditions held no meaning even for the "fogy" who adhered dogmatically to them. Since the animus giving them meaning had died, all that remained were empty husks, symbols without meaning. Dead traditions commanding perfunctory allegiance accounted for the dullness and impassivity which Grierson believed to pervade English life. Under such conditions the artist's imagination could finally be extinguished. Romance and mystery would give way to technological efficiency. "Fogyism" made clear to Grierson that England was a place from which "the soul had departed"; it had became a place "ripe for materialism."[16]

These four indictments can be seen as evidence of Grierson's own eccentricity, of a certain brittleness, a crackling irascibility—characteristics suggesting not only his antipathy toward middle-class society but an exaggerated self-defensiveness about his own position. In other words, it is a rather easy business to pass Grierson off as a crotchety eccentric who is sentimental in his illusions about himself and the world of his imagination and too unrealistic about the condition of his day. Yet it would be unfair to dismiss him so lightly. Moreover, such dismissal would overlook the fact that Grierson does shed light on an era undergoing a radical change. That he made persistent attacks upon contemporary society can be attributed to far more substantial reasons. Of these, three particularly stand out. First, he distrusted democracy and the socialism which he believed would inevitably follow. Second, he was acutely conscious, as he thought the middle class was not, that international tensions would finally explode into world conflict. Third, he feared that, if a materialistic philosophy captured the minds of the intelligentsia, society would lose the enlightened leadership it needed.

On the subject of democracy, Alexis de Tocqueville had observed early in the nineteenth century that a political philosophy agreeable to the wishes of the democratic masses would give people more sovereignty but would also place greater demand upon government to accommodate their newly imagined needs. "Liberty," in a word, "is sacrificed to the demand for equality; and it is the tragedy of a democratic society that the masses are

persuaded to accept the erosion of individuality by the adminis-
tration as a benefit for which they should be grateful."[17]

No direct evidence shows that Grierson had read Tocqueville,
but it is abundantly clear he sympathized with Tocqueville's
analysis of political democracy. To grant rule to the man on the
street, thinking about his own affairs and having little leisure to
reflect on anything else, is admittedly democratic. But Grierson
thought it is not necessarily wise. Involved in his daily routines,
the so-called common man derives values only from his own
experiences; but he makes those values the criteria for judging all
experiences alien to his own. Consequently, as Tocqueville
pointed out, the exceptional man—the uncommon man—is rarely
understood and seldom welcomed because his attitudes are different from those of the crowd and therefore suspect. Such a
person is finally forced to accept the fact of his lost authority.
For individual privilege he must now accept the idea of equality
and social rights, a subtly different point of view. Liberty erodes
into democratic equality. Grierson recognized the distinction between the two, but he held little hope that the democratic masses
ever could or would: "Never under existing conditions [he wrote
in *Parisian Portraits*] will the masses be made to realize the
distinction between social rights and intellectual privileges. . . .
With the ignorant young woman, as with the ignorant young man,
there is no such thing as intellect. . . . The demoralizing notion
that all men are created equal has been doing its work ever since
the French Revolution" (125-26).

Grierson argued that an individual's only political safeguard
was an aristocracy, not necessarily composed of persons with
titles and pedigree but rather of persons—the intelligentsia—who
are exceptionally gifted. In English society he saw no protection
for this latter group. He asserted in *Modern Mysticism* that the
English government was "merging the classes into the masses"
and "the aristocratic into the democratic" (99). Fearing the dis-
appearance of individual privilege, Grierson foresaw only an-
archical collectivism.

Sympathetic with the political conservatives in England, Grierson had reason for alarm. After Gladstone had replaced Disraeli
in 1880, the conservatives led by Lord Salisbury ruled Parliament
only seven of the subsequent thirty-four years before World
War I. Gladstone, a liberal, was the chief figure during much of

this period, although the Independent Labor Party led by Keir Hardie, for whom Grierson had little respect, controlled Parliament during the initial ten years Grierson lived in England. He also thoroughly disliked Hardie's most illustrious admirer, socialist George Bernard Shaw. As for socialism, Grierson thought it a disastrous political and social force.

Grierson did not openly engage in political controversy. Instead, he quietly and resolutely in his essays took the side of W. H. Mallock, the ablest and most prolific literary opponent of socialism. In this position Grierson joined the lingering few, like Hilaire Belloc and G. K. Chesterton, who distrusted democracy and hoped for the eventual recovery of aristocratic society. But unlike them, Grierson never raised his voice loudly enough to draw attack. Shaw, for example, carried on extended warfare with Mallock and others, but Grierson lacked the force to bring Shaw or anyone else down on him. He contented himself with slight essays that were too evanescent for the impact needed in social and political battles.

Yet Grierson remained intransigent in his criticism of England's social temper. He was deeply disturbed by the ambitions of the middle class, mafficking down the primrose paths to the strains of "Ta-ra-ra-boom-de-ay." His concern, all the while, was intensified by the series of crises through which Europe was passing: German claims in Morocco in 1905 and 1911; Austria's annexation of Bosnia in 1908; the Italo-Turkish war in Tripoli in 1911; the Balkan wars in 1912 and 1913; and the Triple Entente of England, France, and Russia which failed to thwart the ambitions of Germany and her partners in the Triple Alliance.

Still more unsettling to Grierson was England's imperialism which he interpreted as the attempt of the power-hungry middle class to maintain its own importance. Though Grierson was never one to disparage Anglo-Saxon supremacy, he did not share John Bull's confidence that progress and profit would continue to bless England. For example, Rudyard Kipling's intoning lines, "Take up the White Man's burden," not only bored Grierson but dispelled any confidence he had left in England's ability to recognize her limitations. In his own way he challenged any view of history which interpreted racial or national life as a steady march toward perfection. He did not view war as a means toward a greater good and certainly not as a justification for an illusory manifest destiny.

Therefore, in light of all these circumstances which to him appeared mounting into gigantic thunderheads, his prediction in *The Invincible Alliance*, published only one year before the start of World War I, is totally prophetic:

> We may be at the beginning of a reign of a state of affairs the like of which the world has never known, a state of things which may cause a pandemonium of unrelenting fury in which all the so-called Christian nations, become materialistic at heart, after playing at hypocrisy so long, will throw off their masks and engage in an Armageddon of slaughter in which the thing called humanity will have no part, in which the total destruction of commercial rivals will be the only incentive and the only aim (137).

Shaken as Grierson was, first by the enfeeblement of England's aristocracy and, second, by the growing international rivalries, he was most profoundly concerned by the pessimism which had darkened the outlook of late nineteenth-century intellectuals. Sufficient to fewer numbers of them was the faith of John Henry Newman in his lines, "Lead kindly light, amid the encircling gloom, lead Thou me on." Matthew Arnold in "Dover Beach" wrote of a coming era with "neither joy, nor love, nor light / Nor certitude, nor peace; nor help for pain." The theme was reiterated by Arthur Hugh Clough, James Thomson, and others; and, by the century's final decade, the melancholic pessimism in A. E. Housman's *A Shropshire Lad* (1896) and the scientific determinism in Thomas Hardy's novels gave little hope to a world where, as Yeats was later to say in "The Second Coming," "Things fall apart; the centre cannot hold."

Furthermore, the impact of Darwinian science with its doctrine of natural selection raised questions about the nature and purpose of man. Darwinian science led to Spencerian sociology. And with the doctrine of the survival of the fittest such a completely new world-view as expressed by Alfred North Whitehead was at hand: "Instead of dwelling on the brotherhood of man, we are now directed to procure the extermination of the unfit."[18] After the Social Darwinists came the historical critics of religion who questioned the divine authority of the Bible and anthropologists like Sir James Frazer who undermined the assumptions of orthodoxy with a new science of comparative religion, which implied that Christianity consisted only of myths analogous to those of primitive religions. Thomas Huxley popularized the term "agnosticism"; Max Nordau played on the theme of degeneration; Freud and Nietzsche studied human irrationality. And so, Francis Grierson—a deeply unsettled conservative, longing for peaceful order and *noblesse oblige*—registered his own fears by declaring in *The Invincible Alliance* that "today nothing but a hatch separates us from primitive barbarism" and that "underneath is the lair of the wild beast, whose growls are as audible and menacing as were those of the old Roman arena when Rome thirsted for human blood" (136). For a moment, Grierson envisioned "a heart of darkness"; or, to use Paul Tillich's metaphor, he felt the shaking of the foundations.

Grierson never really succeeded in putting this vision into artistic form. In *The Valley of Shadows* it is possible to infer some kind of contemporary relevance to the American crisis; but such an inference must remain only the most tenuous kind. The closest Grierson openly came to describing this European pre-war darkness is in the tone of his essays, especially in the essays of *The Invincible Alliance*. At times his irascibility gives way to hysteria, or again to inconsolable frustration and rage. With this tense, erratic tone Grierson does succeed in capturing the mood of an era, given its own character by Auguste Comte's theory that no important distinction separates physical and moral phenomena or, in America, by Charles Sanders Peirce's denial of absolute truth and all metaphysicians' demonstrations of it. It was an era of men scurrying to and fro on an anthill, seeking something to replace their battered certitudes inherited from a century of optimism. Their choice seemed to lie between dumb resignation or rebellion which, if nothing else, would make an end to choice itself. Yet this rebellion, despite its vigor, only hid tacit despair. To the intellectuals, World War I came as the triumph of chaos. A decade later they were fully prepared for Bertrand Russell's solemn and oft-quoted summation that man's life is brief and powerless, and "on him and all his race the slow, sure doom falls pitiless and dark. Blind to good and evil, reckless of destruction, omnipotent matter rolls on its relentless way."[19]

Grierson diagnosed the chief malady in society to be an "agnostic agony" that was caused by a philosophy of materialism holding to no truth but that which positivistic science confirms. The frustration and, finally, the overwhelming futility to which such agony leads was Grierson's explanation for the pessimism among English intellectuals at the end of the century. Grierson himself shared in this frustration, as he watched the days of wine and roses come to an end. But he resisted sharing in the despair. It is at this important point that his philosophic idealism takes over. Beneath his most profound anxiety is the certainty that a pessimist can always find a way out. In the essay "Practical Pessimism" contained in *The Celtic Temperament* Grierson stated that, while modern man seems to know few if any "moments of mystical joy," he nevertheless retains the capacity to experience them. The times are not completely hopeless. Man has an *a priori* capacity to intuit truth beyond what he senses and understands. Grierson illustrated his point by citing examples of the potentially constructive nature of pessimism which sends a person to these most innate and fundamental resources. In the religious pessimism of the Hebrews, the philosophic and poetic pessimism of the Greeks, the stoic pessimism of the Romans, and the mystical pessimism of the early Christians there was affirmed, according to Grierson, a transcendent reality, a realm of absolute truth. Grierson argued that, as in the past, men were able to journey into deep and mystical perceptions illuminating the world beyond, so in the present men could again undertake such a pilgrimage.

CHAPTER *5*

Philosophical Fancies

I *Grierson's Philosophic Stance*

IN HIS BOOK, *The Making of the Modern Mind* (1940), John
Herman Randall, Jr., devotes three chapters to nineteenth-
century influences which shaped the scientific world-view of the
present century. In these chapters certain names appear with
predictable regularity: Sir Charles Lyell, Michael Faraday,
Charles Darwin, Thomas Huxley, Auguste Comte, Herbert Spencer, Ivan Pavlov, Sigmund Freud, Sir Francis Galton, Sir James
Frazer. No less common are such terms as "mechanistic analysis,"
"physical phenomenon," "biological process," and "conditioned
reflex"–plus careful definitions of naturalism, mechanism, and
determinism. Professor Randall also discusses such subjects as
physics, chemistry, biology, geology, anthropology, psychology,
and sociology. In all these terms, points of view, and disciplines
he stresses the singularly common feature–scientific method.
With science as the one point of attention, he makes clear that
in the nineteenth century all thoughtful men had to face the vast
accumulation of scientific knowledge whether to refute it, cele-
brate it, or transcend it.[1]

Necessary though it was for Randall to deal with this scientific
revolution, he also had to treat in a subsequent chapter the
philosophic reactions to it. In this context Grierson took his place
—not in Randall's book but among those persons who, in one way
or another, confronted the new scientific age. Grierson's company
was obviously not among those persons who agreed with Taine
that life was a wonderful scientific and mechanical problem. Nor
did he take sides with those pessimists who, like Schopenhauer,
absorbed the impersonal objectivity of science and then concluded that the essence of nature and life is a dumb, utterly
irrational force called "Will." He likewise eschewed Richard

Wagner's hypnotic theme, as in *Parsifal*, of modern man's re-
nunciation of his will to live. As the great exemplar of pessimism,
Wagner showed Grierson a hopeless *cul de sac;* and he found
Parsifal too depressing, too melancholic: "There is no consolation
in a funeral march." Wagner's entire *Der Ring des Nibelungen*
("Schopenhauer set to music") made "despair triumphant":

> A people who are being schooled in the philosophy of optimistic
> suggestion will refuse to be influenced by the negative and
> lowering moods of the greater part of Wagner's music. The
> suggestive power of *Lohengrin* and *Tannhauser* is little short of
> deadly, to say nothing of the demoralisation set up in the sensi-
> tive listener by a full dramatic representation of *Tristan.* The
> time is at hand when music will be used to heal the mind and
> comfort the heart instead of to fill the mind with melancholy
> and distract the imagination.[2]

Though Grierson was in company with large numbers who
reacted to the world of mechanism and naturalism with its
theories about conservation of energy, laws of thermodynamics,
natural selection, the mechanistic theory of life, and, above all,
an unyielding mechanical determinism, he was not among those
who celebrated this scientific world-view, those who recoiled
from it in inextricable pessimism, or those who surrendered to
the ivory tower of estheticism. Instead, Grierson took his position
in philosophic idealism. Upon this foundation his whole intellectual structure rested.

II *Idealism and Mysticism*

As a social critic Grierson opposed democratic culture which
allowed philistines to win social prominence and power. As a
literary critic he stood firmly against Realism with its emphasis
upon observable commonplaces. As a philosopher—or as one who
held some philosophical fancies—he refuted scientific method as
a means to ultimate knowledge. Writing on all these subjects,
Grierson constantly upheld the notion that behind the human
world of society, art, and understanding were invisible forces
which, if appropriated, could spiritually re-invest the world. This
possibility will be lost, Grierson feared, if the so-called scientific
world-view triumphed. For this reason he insisted that only by
some kind of idealism could modern, de-spiritualized man find
his way out of his agnostic agony.

The peculiar brand of idealism which Grierson espoused was not so much an extension of Platonic philosophy as a reaction against the scepticism of Hobbes, Hume, and Comte—and, in a sense, a turning back to rediscover the spiritual values lost when the scientific revolution upset medievalism. But Grierson was no medievalist. He cared little for the ecclesiastical hierarchy and dogmas of that period, nor was he disposed to identify the spiritual world with the Christian's concept of God. Yet he did turn back to a romantic past which affirmed that the world is governed by spiritual rather than by blindly physical forces. His idealism was similar to the thinking of Kant who had gone to the heart of the problem by seeing that Newtonian science allowed for neither religion nor morality based on freedom. Kant, it will be remembered, argued that in a naturalistic world mechanically governed by gravitation and the laws of motion there remained no place for a dimension of moral order. In the same way, a deterministic world in which every occurrence is the simple result of inexorable causes left no room for free will. But Kant posited a second world, one that was the antithesis of space and time as well as of logical categories of appearances. This was the real world, the world of mind as opposed to the world of matter and physical force. It was a world, he said in his *Theory of Ethics*, that "no human intelligence will ever fathom, but the truth of which, on the other hand, no sophistry will ever wrest from the conviction even of the commonest man."[3]

From Kant's monumental philosophy came post-Kantian idealism which achieved its definitive German statement in Hegel, its English expression with T. H. Green and F. H. Bradley, and its American form in the absolutism of Josiah Royce. While these thinkers did not slavishly follow Kant, they held to presuppositions similar to his. Like Kant, they acknowledged the validity of scientific data in the realm of appearances, but they also asserted that behind this realm lies a different one of spirit. About the nature of this spiritual world they reached no consensus, nor did they agree about how this higher reality could be perceived. They did agree on some basic points about philosophic idealism— even though "idealism" was (and is) a vague, much abused term. First, their philosophy was a reaction against the absolute claims being made by science; second, it posited a transcendental world of spirit; third, it tended to be a conservative force both religiously and socially and became, as Professor Randall points out, the "genteel tradition" in both British and American philosophy.[4]

At this point, a key statement in Grierson's *The Humour of the Underman* reveals his own strong attachment to this philosophical movement. In this passage four central topics stand out: the world of appearance, the world of reality, the method to perceive reality, and the relation between philosophy and esthetics.

> There is a psychic and magnetic correspondence through all things. *Viewed hastily, everything looks like chance; but the deeper we go into the meaning of the things which appear casual, the plainer does the law of phenomenal relativity become.* Perhaps the chief cause of inharmony among people is the ignorance of the world concerning the attractive and the repulsive forces in trivial as well as in great things. *If we could become clairvoyant and psychometric,* the harmonious relation of people and things would become apparent; *colours, sounds, and perfumes would blend in an endless symphony of chromatic tones and tints, and we should recognize law where we now see nothing but chance or chaos* (85-86, italics mine).

Grierson's philosophy presupposes a dualism between the apparent and the real in man, nature, and the cosmos. Man's task is to resolve this dualism—to see through it or beyond it into an essential and monistic reality. In *man* this dichotomy is his "double soul." Emersonian terms describe this condition as the Me and the Not Me. The interior or real Me, which Grierson did not want confused with the merely subconscious mind, acts as the agent by which a person identifies himself with the reality of the cosmic soul and thereby resolves not only his own duality but also that in nature and the cosmos. Grierson thought that discovering this essential Me is difficult because inherent in it, but not quintessential to it, is both a physical and a psychic self, both synonymous with the exterior or non-real self. To yield to the demands of these exterior parts is to move only toward appearances—the ephemeral, chaotic, deceptive, and mysterious. The great difficulty, then, is to bridge the gulf within oneself. This gulf is the widest of all. Not to cross it is to remain with one's own menacing, afflicting, and deadly "exterior." On the other hand, to find successfully one's interior or real soul is simultaneously to discover the reality of both nature and the cosmos.

In *nature* this gulf separating the apparent from the real is not so enormous as the abyss within oneself. Illusions or appearances in nature manifest what Grierson called a "closer relativity" to the real. A person who is sensitive enough—that is, who has discovered his own essential inner reality—is able to perceive this relativity, this "magnetic correspondence," between visible nature and its invisible reality. In other words, nature is deceptive; it shows a false appearance when its observer fails to recognize its analogies with spirit.

In the *cosmos* the dualism consists of the mysterious and the real. Mystery, however, is not radically divorced from the real. Grierson regarded mystery as necessary, if not essential, to it. Far from acting as a menacing or afflicting disturbance, cosmic mystery is both "wonderful" and "subtle." In *The Humour of the Underman* he suggested that if a person can intuit only so far as cosmic mystery he might even there attain the fairest glimpse of "the Eden of serenity" (171).

Mystery is not, however, to be taken for secrecy. "Secrets," he said in the same essay, "are finite sensations and mysteries infinite realities" (170). In deriving ontological significance from mystery, Grierson minimized certain occultistic claims. He believed that, while cognitive knowledge may be secretly experienced, intuited knowledge is not. Philosophically speaking, mystery has nothing to do with Spiritualist mediums swathed in ribbons and seated in darkened séance chambers. Grierson explained to his long-time friend, Claude Bragdon, that visions into cosmic mysteries do not come when a person pays money to a medium, "as if wisdom and inspiration could be bought like coffee."[5] Whether Grierson intended by this comment to place his own Spiritualist practices into question or whether he meant to impugn practitioners less gifted than himself, leaves the reader in that all-too familiar situation of not knowing exactly what Grierson did mean—and of voicing Edmund Wilson's complaint that a good deal of Grierson's writing leaves us "baffled as, for some puzzling reason, we fail to gain access to the author's mind."[6]

The "realm of mist" Wilson later speaks of is, in fact, the same realm of mystery about which Grierson intrepidly tried to conceptualize. In their impressionism his essays do more to convey a sense of this mystery than in their dialectic which, after all, Grierson had neither the temperament nor the philosophical sophistication to write. What frequently saves him from incipience is his inclination to put aside philosophical abstractions, such as those about mystery, and to write about the mysterious evening light in the beautiful Franciscan church of Santa Croce or the deep bell-tones in old Parisian churches.

According to Grierson, we all cannot pierce this mystery which veils spiritual reality, but we do know that without it there would be nothing to compel us to seek beyond it. Mystery excites and intensifies the search for that which we have neither seen, understood, nor fully intuited. As will be noted later, Grierson revered certain French writers who did succeed, strangely, in creating a sense of this mystery in their writing. These writers were the semi-mystical Celts.

As we have seen, Grierson affirmed a supraphenomenal world of spirit. To him there was the one source, the one essence, with an infinite variety of deceptive appearances. The most deceptive appearance was matter itself, and in finally denying the ultimate substantiality of matter, he designated the soul of the cosmos as the only "real idea," the only eternal fixture, which opens to a person only after his internal self resolves the dichotomies in this world and soars through the mysteries to the next. What lies beyond the mysterious mask not even Melville dared to contemplate lest he succumb to the madness borne of a vision of cosmic nothingness. A far less complex man, yet with his own baggage of ambiguities, Grierson said that at the soul of the universe is beauty. Beauty is the cosmic fountainhead, the one force operating in, through, and over all.

At this point Grierson again disappears into the realm of mist. In various places in his writing he juxtaposes beauty with poison, pride, evil, melancholy, and death, as if to suggest that these qualities comprise the mysteries hiding beauty. Because Grierson found this same juxtaposition in Baudelaire's poetry, he was reluctantly drawn to it. For the same reason, he was also attracted to both Poe and Keats who, respectively, linked beauty with the death of a woman and with melancholy. This same mysterious atmosphere Grierson responded to in Chateaubriand's *Mémoires d'Outre-tombe*. To Grierson, beauty obviously was not moralistic sweetness and light, and certainly not something to be understood by common sense which the social middle class prided itself for abundantly possessing. Beauty was metaphysical; its mysteries were best interpreted by those artists and mystics whose inner souls have gained access to its sacred precincts.

How did Grierson propose that this access be gained? As earlier quoted, Grierson said that "If we could become clairvoyant and psychometric ... we should recognize law where we now see nothing but chance or chaos." Ample evidence shows that clairvoyance to Grierson often meant some kind of extra-sensory experience induced in musical séances. In California a few years before his death he seriously thought of inventing a "psychometer" to measure the height and depth of thought and feeling. He also entertained the idea that a person's supposedly electric brain waves enable him to contact sources of energy in nature and to reach another person's spiritual identity. He saw, for example, some likelihood in a genius' cranium being the repository of electro-magnetic energy. Therefore, by means of telepathy such a person could "sit quietly in an obscure corner of the world and launch his psycho-electric currents of thought in a thousand directions" and establish affinities with other geniuses, even if they were deceased.[7]

At a time when such scientists as Cesare Lombroso, Karl Pearson, and Francis Galton were exploring new areas of esoteric knowledge, Grierson took the claims of phrenology seriously. He said that for a person to perceive sublime beauty he must have a "harmonious mind," indicated by the shape of his head. Those persons possessing this kind of mind, he explained in *The Celtic Temperament,* would "have well-rounded heads, and the more irregular the head, the more erratic the mind" (156). These theories comprised much of Grierson's lectures in Los Angeles during his last year when, under the name of "World-Famous Mystic," he spoke to audiences on such subjects as prophecy, vision, cosmic consciousness, and four-dimensional space.

Grierson's occult practices again raise the question of whether he can be taken seriously as a writer and thinker, though he unquestionably took himself so. Does this kind of pseudo-science which Grierson passed off as legitimate practice for a mystic or intuitionist merely show innocuous naïveté? To agree may be to overlook the fact that his interests in occultism during the important years of his literary work were not much different from those same interests of numerous other intellectuals. In America, for example, Orestes Brownson and Margaret Fuller actively inquired into occultism; Nathaniel Hawthorne and

Emerson showed interest in it for a time; Henry James in his story "Professor Fargo" (1874), Oliver Wendell Holmes in *Elsie Venner* (1861), Edward Bellamy in *Looking Backward* (1888), to name but a few writers, were each concerned with some form of occultism, though most of these persons tended to distrust it as a materialistic science.

Actually, occultism at this time touched both Transcendentalism and Neo-Hegelianism. Nineteenth-century idealism fostered a sense of occult forces, intensified by the awakened interest in mental suggestion and in the new cult of mesmerism. The whole American New Thought movement can be seen as a ramification of this interest. The point concerning Grierson is that while he had misgivings when science left the domain of physics, he never completely denied the credibility of intuitional thought-transference. When he returned to the United States from England in 1913 and settled in Los Angeles in 1920, he put aside his reservations about psychical experimentation and yielded completely to what had so long fascinated him.

During his productive years in England it was not down the road of occultism that Grierson traveled in his search for a way to perceive ultimate reality. He had something else in mind when he wrote *Modern Mysticism* which, he said, had "nothing to do with occultism or any of the 'cults' so prevalent now-a-days."[8] Mysticism, variously defined, was Grierson's central concern in his philosophic idealism.

Although mysticism is a tradition within itself, it is closely akin to idealism, if not an extension of it. Both the idealist and the mystic acknowledge a transcendental reality. But, whereas the idealist affirms that truth is attained through rigorous application of speculative logic, the mystic believes in the efficacy of intuitive insight. As an idealist, Grierson outlined a philosophical system, but as a mystic—or as one who wrote, lectured, and played music under this rubric—he went beyond rational and analytical knowledge.

Grierson's mystic way had important markers. The first one was practical experience, the kind which supposedly takes a person into far-off lands and demands of him vigorous psychic energies, such as those Grierson said he exerted as he made his way through the salons and courts of Europe. To attain personal independence by means of these psychic resources marks the completion of this first step. The next step is the development of

intuitional power, To Grierson this achievement comes only to
the person who is at least thirty years old. Grierson's point has
interesting validity, for many writers have shown this age to be
crucial in a person's spiritual development. One thinks of Fitz-
gerald's Nick Carraway, Kafka's Joseph K., and Mann's Little
Herr Friedemann, to name but three characters in fiction whose
thirtieth birthday brought on a personal revolution in psychic
perspective. Carl Jung in his *Modern Man in Search of a Soul*
(1933) gives similar importance to this age at which a person
confronts himself as he is and not as he imagines he will become. With Grierson there is none of the existential drama which
modern novelists have brought to this age of a person's life.
Moreover, Grierson lived before *angst* became "popular." Yet
he does regard this period of life as peculiarly important to a
person's inner condition.

The next requirement is disciplined introspection, meaning
that as intuition turns inward a person is brought to a point of
severe self-scrutiny enabling him to purge his chaotic desires.
Here Grierson calls for a renunciation of everything earthly in
order that one can touch the wellsprings of spiritual power. This
purgation demands the act of mortification. "To develop a spirit
of indifference," he wrote in *La Vie et les Hommes*, "it is necessary that I destroy in myself all sensations of jealousy, envy,
pride" (58-59). It is an act of becoming selfless in order to realize
one's real selfhood or spiritual identification. Grierson at this
point is echoing Eastern mysticism which has had its modern
American spokesmen, especially in California, authoritatively
represented on the one hand by Aldous Huxley's perennial philosophy and, on the other, by crack-brained Los Angeles
astrophilogics.

In only a few places does Grierson attempt to describe the
mystical moment. In *The Valley of Shadows* he places much
importance upon "silences" that belonged to the prairies and to
the preacher and prophet whose voices announced that more
than a national crisis was at hand. Because of their age and wisdom, and their long-practiced indifference to things of this world,
they saw beyond the events of the day a great spiritual power
shaping the destiny of all men for all time. In this book Grierson
displayed rare sensitivity for this mystical dimension and for
those persons living under its penumbra. In his essays he was less
successful. Yet as one critic pointed out, it was remarkable

enough that anyone should even attempt to describe mystical experience at a time when modern man was enslaved by the "great God Commonsense."[9] In two passages from *Modern Mysticism* Grierson suggests that to achieve this mystical experience completes the supreme quest:

> Mysticism is the astronomy of the soul; and a mystical mind is an intellectual telescope probing for specks of truth in a universe of eternal mystery. The non-mystical is dissipated by centrifugal force; but mystical thought is centripetal in its action, ever aspiring towards the central and the ideal. . . . No sooner does poetic intuition penetrate to a new conception of Nature's enigma than the mind becomes conscious of revolving inside a new circle of unsolved problems. Paradox and illusion are the riddles, the tempters, and the tormenters of the poets, for the deeper the soundings the more imperative the mystery (15).

> . . . .

> While the body goes its own way, passing from one grade of life to another, the mind has its own mode of progress unknown to superficial observers. . . . This is the immortal part of us. The mystical element in man to-day is as real and perennial as the mysticism of Athens and Jerusalem (16).

As an extension of philosophic idealism, Grierson's "modern mysticism" was, therefore, still another reply to modern science which was breaking down the older conception of reality. Grierson saw that scientific positivism had undermined an *a priori* universal order; and, as sincerely as Galileo, Kepler, Newton, and later scientists attempted to palliate laymen by conceiving a larger synthesis by which to unify the multiplicity and complexity their inductive method had exposed, the Baconian law—as Henry Adams in his *Education* pointed out—still held fast. Instead of thought evolving nature, nature evolved thought. Adams described a time when once "man held the highest idea of himself as a unit in a unified universe," a condition attributable to the "occult attraction" men experienced between 1150 and 1250 A.D. toward the all-powerful, all-authoritative, coalescing force of the Virgin.[10] This force in the new twentieth century seemed remote to Adams, just as it did to Grierson. Hoping for a resurgence of philosophic idealism, Grierson looked to the future with tempered optimism. For himself, idealism was the philosophical basis for the mysticism he claimed to practice. It is in this context that his views on esthetics should be understood.

III *Esthetics*

From the idealist's assertion that the essence of reality is spirit and from the mystic's belief that this spiritual reality is accessible by means of intuitive apprehension, Grierson developed his own esthetic theories. Again the impelling force behind them was rebellion against a positivistic theory of art. What Grierson saw in the positivists was their failure to distinguish the activity called "artistic" from the activity called "scientific." Not only had they failed to explain beauty but they had taken no account of the values related to it. As a philosophy, positivism paid little attention to artistic genius, and it classified art in no other way but according to the human origins involved in one's response to it. Grierson was critical of all these shortcomings but, most emphatically, with those relating to genius and beauty.

His ideas about the special qualities of genius contributed importantly to many of his philosophical essays. These special qualities Grierson swelled to archetypal patterns, whether he was writing about prairie seers or about great poets. He described such geniuses as persons displaying a broad, active sympathy with all that lives. They possess "a sense of tears in mortal things, beneath all a substratum of passion, above all a region where imagination conceives and creates" (*The Humour of the Underman*, 64). Deep feeling is their essential hallmark, a depth of feeling which penetrates to the soul of creation. No one lacking this capacity can approach the mysteries of life, to say nothing of going beyond them. If, however, a person lives in this dimension of mystery and, moreover, has the imagination to conceive artistic expression in it, then he possesses the genius of a poet. His consummate refinement enables him to see "aesthetic correspondence" between the supernal order of beauty and its analogies in the visible world. In other words, the genius is both mystic and artist. Only the genius, as mystic-artist, can see into and beyond the mysteries, and only he can translate his vision into artistic form.

The combination of poet and mystic brings strange results, strange in that such a person's art miraculously harmonizes all discordant tensions. In Grierson's view, only an artistic genius has the imaginative power to bring these tensions into artistic unity. The process of this production requires both the mystic's insight and the artist's shaping imagination. Such a person in

whom the combination dynamically operates fits Shelley's definition of a poet in "A Defense of Poetry" as a person who par-
ticipates "in the eternal, the infinite, and the one" and becomes
"an instrument over which external and internal impressions
are driven."[11]

Grierson believed that in this heightened capacity a poet relates
himself to all objects and to their ideal or transcendent reality.
At such a moment he loses his own identity and absorbs the total
object. This moment of subliminal perception—associated not
with esoteric occultism but with what Grierson repeatedly called
"poetic instinct"—reveals essential beauty in all objects. To Grierson, this intimacy with beauty marks the genius. His art which
has touched this metaphysical beauty becomes something akin to
religious expression which, to Grierson, characterizes all supreme
art. The artist's prime motive is religious because he seeks to
transcend time by imbuing the commonplace with an eternal
presentness.

Grierson's ideas on esthetics extend from his presuppositions
about both idealism and mysticism. Mysticism affected esthetics
by giving to the mystic an explanation of why he finds art valu-
able at all. An esthetic experience is a way to apprehend the
agencies of the invisible world. Art serves as a link between
appearance and reality or, in Grierson's terms, as "a complete
union ... between the material and the spiritual" (*The Humour
of the Underman*, 202). Because the affective aspect of art exists
quite independently of the imitative, one is able through art to
find the stuff of reality, namely beauty. Using the arguments of
Plotinus, who averred that art does not go back merely to nature
but to the ideas antecedent to nature, Grierson recognized in
art something divine in its esthetical correspondence with absolute beauty. Echoing Carlyle's statements in the third book of
Sartor Resartus, Grierson conceived the intrinsic value of art to
lie in its rendering more visible the nature of the godhead which
to Grierson was beauty.

As Grierson stressed in *Modern Mysticism*, the artist's duty is
not to preach ("philosophical systems are no longer tolerable")
but "to give a spiritualized pleasure"—to put chaotic dreams and
reveries into perfect form, and to aim solely for the harmony of
beauty (126). Grierson did not imply that "pleasure" belongs to
the class of pleasures which satisfies physiological needs or gives
vicarious, sensuous thrills. By pleasure Grierson meant a kind of

mystical ecstasy culminating in one's recognition of ideal beauty. The artist, therefore, mediates between two worlds and reconciles their dualism. Should his eye strike upon the slums of Liverpool or upon the depravity of a French peasant family, he accepts these phenomena within the perspective of spiritual beauty and reality.

In Grierson's scheme of things the poet, for all his mystical power, finally takes second place to the musician. Calling music a "psychic necessity," Grierson said in *The Invincible Alliance* that music is the last refuge against "the onslaughts of materialism" (114). More than poetry, music absorbs the "harmonic vibrations" of beauty. It is the one universal art because it is the most metaphysical of all the arts. It awakens the soul, Grierson said; it renders the soul clairvoyant and therefore makes possible the dissolution of mystery itself. The exaltation which such clairvoyance inspires comes only to the person who has passed through "the magic circle of sounds" (*Parisian Portraits,* 162). The artist having the most mystical authority is, therefore, the musician under whose leadership in the rebellion against materialism will come a union of music, literature, and philosophy, but music will be the key to all.

Grierson's ideas on the metaphysics of music are not to be found in any one essay or book he wrote. In one way or another, they permeate most of his philosophical expression. As we have noted, Grierson's spirit world was one of a transcendent and entirely spiritualized beauty. But most importantly, this ontological beauty was itself inaudible music, a kind of musical stirring with no words, no sounds, and audible only to the mystic's soul. Grierson's conception of music is aptly described in Wallace Stevens' line from "Peter Quince at the Clavier"—"Music is a feeling then, not a sound." Music comes before thought and words, and it extends beyond them. It is the innate source of all art and all emotion. A man who lacks music in his soul, as Coleridge said in Chapter XV of *Biographia Literaria,* can never be a "genuine poet."

Holding to these views, Grierson used his mediumistic talents to good advantage as he sought to sweep his listeners into the vortex of musical emotion and to awaken them to what in his day was popularly called "cosmic consciousness," a term that came from the title of Richard Maurice Bucke's book published in 1901. But Grierson had behind him far more substantial authorities than Bucke. For at the turn of the century, when music did occupy a dominant position among the arts, Henri Bergson had already worked out his elaborate theory of time (*la durée*) in *Essai sur les données immédiates de la conscience* (1888), maintaining in this book that music was the most immediate and intuitionally felt of esthetic form because it was a time-art as distinguished from literature, which he said was a space-art. Then there was also the example of Richard Wagner whose spellbinding success in uniting poetry and music inspired a Wagner cult who religiously read the *Revue Wagnerienne,* a periodical founded and supported by the composer's followers whose admiration rested on the metaphysical argument that musical feeling is idealism at its best.[12]

Still another illustration giving perspective to Grierson's views on music comes from French Symbolist poets who, like Rimbaud and Mallarmé, were influenced by Wagner's manner of combining music and libretto in continuous recitative. These poets claimed to touch some inner source —"either expressive, or emotive, or mystical"—which brought their poetry closer to music than to anything else.[13] They aimed for poetic purity that spiritualized literature, and in this effort they spoke in terms of the "instrumentation" of poetic cadences and resolutions. It was said of Mallarmé that "his was the art of bringing verse to the song of an orchestra" and that his poem "Apres-midi d'un Faun" amounted to "visible music."[14] As Edmund Wilson explained in *Axel's Castle* (1931), the Symbolists made their words approximate the "indefiniteness" of music.[15] Esthetes in England who followed the same ideal placed much importance upon Walter Pater's dictum that "all art aspires towards the condition of music."[16] Among all these writers, literature was a kind of musical symbol. To Grierson, music was the highest artistic achievement. It was literature, philosophy, and all experience spiritualized. It was liberation from agnostic agony and despair.

CHAPTER 6

The Altar of Art

I *Realism and Its Milieu*

S TRONGLY COLORED by metaphysical overtones, Grierson's views on literature vigorously opposed the Realism of his day which, in France, took its theoretical ideas from the writings of Auguste Comte, Claude Bernard, and Hippolyte Taine. Before their time the champion of idealism had been Victor Cousin whose published lecture-courses of 1816-1819 and *Fragments philosophiques* (1826) had introduced German Transcendentalism to France. But Cousin's eclectic school of idealism failed to withstand the onslaught of Comte who elevated scientific study far above theological and metaphysical inquiry. His six-volume *Cours de philosophie positive* (1830-1842) firmly planted his positivistic ideas in France. His ideas were not seriously challenged until Schopenhauer gained belated popularity around 1870 and until Bergson published *Essai sur les données immédiates de la conscience* in 1889.

According to Comte's positivism, the artistic role was only to embellish life and never in any way to direct it in matters of social or political action. Comte held that artists have certain inherent defects which make their work an unreliable and, fundamentally, invalid guide in matters of human understanding. The main defect is their subordination of reason to imagination, a fault corrected only by systematic education. Claude Bernard appeared later to specify the techniques which such an education would perfect. In his *Introduction a l'étude de la medice expérimentale* (1865), which positivists considered a supreme discourse on method, Bernard explained how the techniques of empiricism and experimentation conduct researchers to final truth about all natural phenomena. Underlying Bernard's thesis was the presupposition that life is reducible to scientific laws which someday would yield complete knowledge to reasoning man. The key idea in this important book is simply stated: "If I had to define life in a single phrase... I should say: life is creation... we have not yet been able to reduce it to physicochemical terms; but in that we shall doubtless succeed some day."[1] To Hippolyte Taine, another positivist, all phenomena are understandable when a person discovers causal dependencies. Courage, ambition, or love, for example, can be explained when one learns their causes. This task entails a careful investigation of psychological and sociological facts. Regarding a human being as a predictably functioning mechanism, Taine thought that piecing facts together led to a complete picture of man, the sum of his hereditary and environmental legacy. Central in his *De l'intelligence* (1870) was Taine's notion that all small facts constitute the material of science.

These three men and their followers built an intellectual front so formidable that the cause of idealism was all but lost. Writing in *La Metaphysique et son avenir* (1860) on the general state of philosophy in France, Ernest Renan believed that metaphysical speculation in the tradition of Kant, Hegel, and Cousin was not likely to continue because the positivists had successfully established two important ideas. The first was that ultimate knowledge could never be reached by philosophy. The second was that bankrupt philosophy must now yield to the ascendency of science. The intellectual temper Grierson first encountered in France was scientific rather than metaphysical; its energies were directed toward accumulating, experimenting, and testing facts rather than seeking their spiritual analogues.

Taking their cue from the positivists, Realists thought of art as an exact reproduction of nature, devoid of any necessary connection with beauty as a philosophical ideal. Art was to be a strictly photographic imitation of contemporary life and its surfaces. Myth was to be replaced by observable facts wherein truth was supposedly to be found. After 1857 the words *réalisme* and *réaliste* appeared in almost every literary discussion.[2] The lines of scientific positivism and literary Realism kept apace until, in 1863, they converged with the publication of Taine's *Histoire de la littérature anglaise* which presented in the famous Introduction the theory that the laws of art relate to the scientific laws of society, and that the social forces of Race, Surroundings, and Epoch shape art much as the weather works on a pear tree. The artist uses material presented to his senses and then intellectually interprets it before he concerns himself with the artistic significance or the essential character of the material itself. Furthermore, the artist intellectually decides what he ought to emphasize rather than emotionally feels what he must emphasize. The critic, likewise, must base his judgment upon strictly intellectual, scientific analysis. Taine argued that the critic's personal taste has no value, that he must set aside his temperament, inclination, party, and interests. Only then could he engage in literary analysis which, at its best, resembles a scientific operation, capable of verification and perfectibility.[3] Such a theory depends for its authority upon positivistic sociology. Taine supplied this foundation in his elaborate *Philosophie de l'art* in 1865, four years before Grierson arrived on the Continent.

In recent years Jacques Maritain, among many other writers, has attempted to show how short of the mark fall such explanations of art as offered by "psychological or sociological, materialist, empiricist, logical-empiricist, or pragmatist positivism."[4] In his discussion he cites Allen Tate's objections to positivistic theories of art which purport to explain, writes Tate in *On the Limits of Poetry*, "how the *stimuli* of poems elicit *responses* in such a way as to *organize our impulses* toward action," as if one were to suppose that "poetry is a kind of applied psychology" or "is only *amiable insanity*" because "it 'designates' but does not denote anything *real*."[5]

In his day, however, Grierson saw that, as the nineteenth century waned, Realism founded on these tenacious assumptions of positivism changed into the more depressing Naturalism and, with it, an even more doctrinaire extension of pseudo-scientific principles. He abhorred the Naturalists' literary emphasis upon the conflict of social forces and, worse yet, upon the sordid, shocking, and depressive aspects of existence. With the Rougon-Macquart series of Zola highlighted by such novels as *L'Assommoir, Nana, Germinal,* and *La Terre;* with the novels of the Goncourt brothers, J. K. Huysmans, de Maupassant, and the so-called "putrid literature" of the Germinie Lacerteux school; and with the culmination of Realism and Naturalism in the morbid decadence of the *fin de siècle* which proclaimed, with Jules Laforge, the "eternullity" of life—with all these came Grierson's still small but protesting voice.

The larger protests came from the French Parnassians and

Symbolists, led by Leconte de Lisle and Stéphane Mallarmé. They were joined by Neo-Romantics who, like Edmond Rostand, rediscovered the historic past and, like Pierre Loti, wrote stories about remote, exotic lands. In England the Pre-Raphaelites including the esthetes of the 1890's waged battle. A few Americans followed later, notably Edgar Saltus, Lafcadio Hearn, and James Huneker. A broader reaction came early in the twentieth century with the novels of Marcel Proust, James Joyce, Virginia Woolf, Dorothy Richardson, and Henry James. Each owed a debt to Henri Bergson whose philosophy directly opposed positivism. In such works as *Essai sur les données immédiates de la conscience, L'Evolution creative* (1907) and *L'Energie spirituelle* (1919), Bergson sought to establish reliance upon intuition and to foster impulse and emotion as creative resources. Writers thereafter found a new freedom in artistic method, for it was Bergson who gave importance to the indeterminate, symbolic, mythical, and incoherent.

This introductory discussion hardly covers the range of literary activity at this time. Its purpose is merely to show that concurrent with Grierson there was a substantial literary reaction taking shape against positivistic Realism.

II *Grierson's Opposition to Realism*

Grierson leveled four specific charges against French Realism. First, he said that writers who accepted the presuppositions of positivism turned man into a trivial machine divorced from all communion with spiritual reality. These writers of so-called Realism discount mystery, as if mystery and truth were mutually exclusive and only awaited the scientist to dispose of the one and prove the other. The Realists look upon life, Grierson said, as a detective problem which awaits a complete solution. Beauty and mystery are nothing more than intellectual problems for rational understanding, both losing their metaphysical importance in an epistemology which finds its methods in the laboratory. Truth as unchanging and eternal is, therefore, fashioned away by the observations of the day.

His second indictment, most forcefully given in "La Révolte Idéaliste," called Realistic literature a "materialistic art," a "battle of intellectuality," powerless to elevate the reader in true knowledge and forceful only in "bruising his head and hurting his heart" (*Pensées et Essais,* 72). Comparing modern Realism to problems in algebra, Grierson thought it artistic suicide to favor facts over their inherent essence. He argued that only the imaginative (Romantic) artist bridges the two, thereby avoiding unwarranted attention to facts alone. Grierson charged that the Realists were too precise, too photographic (he grew weary of Zola's word pictures), and that, while they ought to go beyond literal details to spiritualized emotion, they instead remained with superficialities.

Grierson wanted the artist to be aware of two levels of existence, the one analogous with the other. But the passion for objectivity, for reporting facts rather than seeing them as emblematic of higher truth, Grierson found destructive to the whole artistic process. Of course, Grierson failed to understand that the Realist's objectivity was itself controlled by both subjective and esthetic purposes. Grierson's position, however, is clear. He aligned himself with those critics of Realism who declared, with corrosive irony: "Copy reality, transcribe it literally, such are the supreme conditions of art, all the rest is error; that is to say, do not feel, do not think, do not mediate, restrain your heart, extinguish your intelligence, deaden your taste, make of your brain an object of photography, and all will be well."[6]

Grierson's third objection was against the subject matter chosen by Realists. He considered the everyday affairs of people either too dull or too shocking to include in literature. Taken alone, these mundane details offered Grierson less than the smiling aspects of life; moreover, Grierson thought them to be deadening to life itself. He compared reading Zola's novels, for example, to listening to an organ's roaring low tones which torture the nerves and leave one shouting "no more!"

Finally, Grierson found French Realism lacking in beauty. He saw no possibility for beauty when the subject matter itself lacked it or, more accurately, when writers looked at their subject as itself a dead end. What he wanted was release from this kind of bondage. Echoing Hawthorne's theory of Romance in the Preface to *The House of the Seven Gables,* he conceived of beauty as that quality which emerges from literature when the artist has infused his materials with touches of supernatural and spiritual wonder. Hardly in agreement with Hawthorne as to the psychological results of such technique, Grierson argued that this kind of art leads to joy and serenity. In Realism he found much to shatter feelings but nothing to bring back calm and repose, and certainly nothing to inspire mystical illumination. Regarding Realism as devoid of beauty, Grierson closed his case against the predominant type of French, English, and American literature at the end of the century.

Curiously enough, Grierson lacked sympathy with many of his own literary allies. He repeatedly criticized the Parnassians for their pedantry. He thought that the poetry of Leconte de Lisle displayed inordinate concern for brilliant but dispassionate beauty. (He found the man himself vain, nervous, self-conscious, and dull, and his salon entirely uninteresting.) As for the Symbolists, Grierson was bedazzled to the point of confusion, charging that, because their poetry was too "angular," he was led into a kind of mystical chaos. Most curiously, he betrayed patent dilettantism by admitting in *Modern Mysticism* that he could not make head nor tail out of Mallarmé's poetry, but he frequently delighted in affirming to share Mallarmé's outlook and intentions. Among the English rebels of Realism, specifically the "art-for-art's-sake" school, Grierson found excessive flamboyance and personal license. For all of Oscar Wilde's wit and technical skill, Grierson thought he lacked depth; he added that, at a time when Neo-Romanticism needed crusaders, the behavior and persiflage of the esthetes only proved to the positivists that Romanticism had no relevance to a materialistic society.

Clearly, Grierson himself was no innovator. His ideas came largely from sources in the contemporary rebellion against Realism as it flourished especially in France. The irony of Grierson's position is that he failed to understand the full meaning of those writers on whose side he claimed allegiance. The important work of Henry James or, in France, of the Symbolist poets left him standing on its periphery, befuddled as to the deeper psychological realism which these writers presented. Grierson saw himself as a preserver of the old traditions of Romanticism, though to preserve them he was stylistically far more the Classicist. His essays are sometimes like frosty icicles. With his diamond tie-pin and ruby rings in assertive predominance and with every hair of his moustache waxed in place, Grierson stood apart too often as a *poseur* who was unwilling to appreciate the tragic agony of others and the realists' efforts to capture this condition. Instead, he maintained his Byronic stance, unaware of its pretensions. Always implicit in his literary theories was a vision—

both private and precious—of the artist as aristocrat. Grierson's rebellion against new literary movements grew from his fear that aristocracy had become anachronistic. By extension, he saw the same fate for art. But a more telling fate, for himself, was that his aristocratic aloofness kept him from fully participating in the life around him. Therefore, his ideas about it and about its literature lack the sinew to make them convincing. Too often his bloodless essays give the impression that their author was some disembodied spirit whose return to corporeality, even through a Realist's hearty grunt or guffaw, the reader would greatly cheer.

III *Theories About Art and Language*

Grierson's literary criticism consists, however, of more than rebellion against Realism. As noted in the preceding chapter, he developed his esthetics within the context of idealism and mysticism. He believed that the artist should aim solely toward ideal beauty, the worth of his art diminishing in proportion to his misguided effort to create either an intellectual system or realistic detail. In short, the best art points to another world rather than analyzing or photographing the present one. Because Zola's *La Terre*, for example, realistically gives a picture of French peasant life, Grierson held that the novel is unfortunately limited to only these self-contained details. By contrast, Edgar Allan Poe's *Eureka*, while grossly inaccurate in matters of natural science, is higher art to Grierson because Poe succeeded in creating impressions which suggest a larger reality. Accordingly, Poe's art expresses a greater degree of artistic beauty.

This dubious logic led Grierson to assert that the poet must be a mystic, for it is only through mystical apprehension of beauty that he can create an impression of it. Art ceases to be a technique and becomes a religion. All the forces of will and reason momentarily subside as the artist loses his self-identity in this apprehension. His art is little else than the remembrance of this moment.

Grierson knew what he wanted in a literary theory. In the dilemma between positivism and the revival of mystical idealism, he chose the latter. Like many artists of his day, he found in this direction an unrestricted range of expression, one free from the pseudo-scientific limitations imposed by Realism. At the same time Bergson's theories on intuitions,[7] which required a stripping off of intellectuality, gave new authority to a person such as Grierson who held that through intuition and feeling an artist achieves mystical insights. The French critic Charles Morice persistently relied upon mystical arguments to assert art's supremacy over all other human creations.[8] Furthermore, as Albert Beguin illustrates in his essay on "Poetry and Occultism," many French literary contemporaries of Grierson were influenced by occult sources, namely Swedenborgian currents and the Jewish Cabala, both proclaiming mystical art as the way to the infinite.[9] In short, much of nineteenth-century French literature from Chateaubriand to Balzac, even with the emergence of Realism, is subtly threaded by mysticism.

The important point is that mysticism gave Grierson an explanation of why literature was unique. This explanation took the form of Carlyle's assertion in *Sartor Resartus* that in the esthetic experience a person is brought into more or less direct communication with the infinite, be it Nature, God, or Beauty.

Some critics called this kind of speculation nonsense. One such outspoken dissenter was Max Nordau, considered by his contemporaries to be a Jeremiah of doom and disaster. In his lugubriously entitled book, *Degeneration,* he made great pronouncements against French Symbolism which he termed "degeneracy and imbecility," presumably caused in part by its adoption of esthetic mysticism. The Symbolists showed Nordau only "incoherent cackle" and "incoherent mysticism." He attacked what he thought was their basic fallacy: that the main purpose of art is to leave the reader with impressions which his own imagination can privately verify. Nordau took no stock in this idea, nor in any claim that through artistic impressionism a reader can transcend intellectuality and thereby reach a higher plain of truth. In referring specifically to Maeterlinck's dramas, Nordau said that this kind of impressionism takes one into an "utterly childish idiotically-incoherent mysticism."[10]

Despite the Nordaus, the Taines, and the Zolas, Grierson never displaced his conviction that the creative impulse behind all art is intuitive, mystical, extra-sensory. Another of Grierson's assertions pertains to language. He conceived of language as organic, combining both thought and form into dynamic mutuality. Perfect language is the natural expression of an idea. When it is most eloquent, it corresponds naturally to the essential simplicity common to all final wisdom.[11]

This theory reminds one of Schlegel and other German Romanticists who suggested that the inner force in nature determines its outward form in much the same way that the vitality of an artist's intuition shapes its own appropriate expression. "Such as the life is, such is the form" was Coleridge's dictum, and it was followed later in the century by Walter Pater's *Appreciations* in which he defined literary art as the external form of "soul fact." The Concord philosophers held to a similar organic principle in art; Emerson in his essay "The Poet" presented the theory and Thoreau in *Walden* consummately illustrated it.[12]

Grierson wanted words to be sentient but grew uneasy if they seemed too vague. When, for example, Mallarmé suggested that a word may hardly depend at all upon its objective meaning, Grierson feared that with such autonomy language would disintegrate into formlessness. When a poem is so subjectively conceived as to be unintelligible or even obscure, or when its form so radically violates the conventional patterns that readers resist it, then Grierson questioned the legitimacy of innovation. He insisted that words be natural, by which he meant that they be free from twisted and oblique ambiguities. His simplistic view of reality demanded a similar kind of language. This language he called "natural"; but, in view of his remarkable success with dialect in *The Valley of Shadows*, he might better have called it "authentic" or "regional." What he looked for was a philosophic explanation of language itself. Indebted to Emerson, whose essays he read with deep appreciation, Grierson thought of language as organically related to nature and to nature's truth. And this truth he found to be profoundly simple.

From this theory of language came Grierson's predilection for both aphorism and the concise essay. He considered these forms of expression to be consistent with the simple profundity he intended them to convey. Something perceived intuitively needed no long-winded exposition; the short, quick statement was its best medium. He claimed that the aphorism strikes deeply and immediately to the center of an idea. Much like Poe's objection to long epic poetry, Grierson considered it unreasonable that a long work treat a subject understood initially in a flash of sudden illumination. For this reason, he felt that Balzac and Tolstoy dissipated too much energy in writing inordinately long and numerous books. He thought Carlyle would have improved

Sartor Resartus if he had condensed it to fifteen pages. Grierson's touchstone was so-called natural and aphoristic expression, taking its form from the intuited ideas first compelling it. This expression—distilled, condensed, polished—Grierson described in *The Humour of the Underman* as "the quintessential element of art" (164).

Accordingly, Grierson considered the aphorism essential to literature of power, the term used by Thomas De Quincey whose *Confessions of an English Opium Eater* Grierson regarded as one of the finest works in English literature. To Grierson, the power of literature lies in its concentration and precision. This quality he found superbly displayed in Emerson's aphoristic essays, tightly compounded of imagination and precision, perfect in themselves; and in their perfection they achieved an extraordinary depth which struck at the very heart of the matter. Old Testament prophets also illustrated the "fine frenzy" contained in aphorism. Concentrated energy was the real secret to the final triumph of language. Convinced of the power of the aphorism, Grierson repeatedly described it with imagery of lightning: the aphorism "penetrates," "illuminates," "flashes"; it is "light" and "electricity."

One need not argue with Grierson that an aphorism is good when it distills long experience and reflection. The trouble is that aphorisms can also be easily manufactured. An idea may in fact be much too complex to be summarized in a single, neat expression. Irwin Edman has warned that, because aphorisms have an air of finality and moral tone, they may only serve to hide a "quick, evanescent piece of cracked wisdom."[13] He could have added that too many aphorisms at one time exhaust the reader or, worse, bore him. Grierson would have granted both possibilities. Nevertheless, the well-turned, epigrammatic statement has its legitimate use, and in literary history has unquestionably had its masters. In Grierson's day, Oscar Wilde spun out aphoristic filigree, to say nothing of Nietzsche's lightning bolts. For Grierson, the aphorism was a way to get things said with authority.

Of curious interest is one obscure publication which he entitled *Some Thoughts,* a pamphlet containing thirty-two aphorisms extracted from his previous writing. From among the following aphorisms, which fairly represent the pamphlet, it is clear that Edman's point has some validity.

New talent has two worlds to conquer—the material within and the material without.

. . . .

The soul is an eternal reality.

. . . .

Ninety parts of all inexplicable phenomena have their source in the interior doubles.

. . . .

The clearest seers are the artists.

. . . .

We must be able to see before we can create.

. . . .

Mere invention does not make the artist.

. . . .

Nature is never in a hurry. Artists and thinkers must learn at the outset the inexorable truth that the finest faculties develop slowly.

. . . .

Science contains as much superstition as is manifest by any form of belief known to the world.

. . . .

Before we affirm let us be certain our affirmation be not founded on illusion.

. . . .

Power comes from within.

. . . .

Genius is affirmation.[14]

In trying to adapt his organic theory of language to his own aphorisms and short essays, Grierson sought conciseness and even sublimity but often ended only in vagueness. Many of his essays cry out for more detail. But rather than supply this elaboration, he sent his arrows directly to what he thought was the core of an idea. Not only, therefore, are his essays brief, sometimes only three hundred words or so, but his individual sentences snap shut as if the final word has been said. This kind of style has inherent dangers which Grierson failed to avoid. When aphorisms bear too much generalized freight, when they presumably sum up complex social and philosophical questions, their conciseness may turn into vagueness and their sublimity into bathos. When less than brilliant, aphorisms become painfully didactic and precious. Had Grierson more often loosened his style and then amplified his ideas, he would have achieved the authoritative tone which readers could trust and which he himself so dearly treasured. Instead, as with practically everything Grierson did, certain misgivings lurked in the minds of persons who followed his work. Assuredly the critic who said that Grierson's writing had "conciseness," "concentration of style," and "unusual force" spoke for many of Grierson's readers, but not for all. The other critic who called him an "affectatious" spinner of epigrams touched the other side of his personality and career which readers could never quite forget.[15]

IV *Literary Kinships*

Grierson used his theories to appraise the work of literary contemporaries, not all of whom in his judgment were as contemptible as the Realists. Passing over the English esthetes and French Symbolists whom he considered too flamboyant and experimental, respectively, he searched and found certain other writers representing his own brand of eloquence and truth. From them and from his own company among them he devoutly hoped for a spiritual renaissance in literature.

The first of these writers was Pierre Loti (pseudonym of Louis Marie Julien Viaud) upon whom Grierson bestowed the generous accolade "acceptable" (*Parisian Portraits,* 65). Though he had reservations about Loti's somewhat too pagan Neopaganism in several of his books, Grierson could not shake the deep impression made upon him by Loti's *Pêcheurs d'Islande.* To Grierson, this particular book showed the author's uncanny power to describe silent impressions and to transmit feelings. The chord touching Grierson most keenly in the work was the Celtic temperament of the Breton fishermen whose stillness and mystery contrasted with the violence and coldness of the rugged Icelandic coast. The psychic resources of these men Grierson interpreted as a defense against the harsh realities of their occupation and life. This quality of calm patience, of dreamy mysticism was what he found unique to the Celtic temperament; and, for him, Pierre Loti had successfully captured it. Loti had not been the chief inspiration behind the renewed interest in Celtic culture, but Grierson acknowledged his contribution to it. Of more importance

were two other writers, Ernest Renan and François Chauteau-
briand.

A word needs to be said about this Celtic revival which Grierson predicted would play an important role in the Neo-Romantic
movement. Holbrook Jackson noted that somewhere around 1856
Ernest Renan discovered the Celt.[16] He cited Renan's *The Poetry
of the Celtic Races* in which Renan—himself a Breton with a
deep substratum of the Celtic spirit—wrote that "sufficient attention is not given to the peculiarity of this fact of an ancient race
living, until our days and almost under our eyes, its own life in
some islands and peninsulas in the West." Renan then described
the character of these people and their poetry. He found a sadness, a delicacy and depth of feeling, and a great imaginative
power; and he concluded that "we are far from believing that
this race has said its last word."[17]

As early as the 1850's scholars in Britain were translating
Celtic texts.[18] With the publication of Yeats's first book of poems
in 1885 and *The Wanderings of Oisin, and Other Poems* in 1889
the Celtic revival attained genuine significance. Further impetus
from Scotland came in Patrick Geddes' four numbers of the
Evergreen in 1895 and 1896 which featured William Sharp (Fiona
Macleod) whose work bore the characteristics of mystical Celtic
aloofness. But Grierson was more concerned with the Celtic
movement in France than in England.

More specifically, it was in the writings of François Chateaubriand who, like Renan, was born in a Breton town (St. Malo),
that Grierson discovered "the Celtic temperament in all its
complex charm, mystical depth, and that indefinable something
which hovers over and around the real and the commonplace"
(*The Celtic Temperament,* 30). In the essay on the Celtic temperament from which his book takes its title, Grierson described
not only Chateaubriand and the Celtic quality in literature but
also the peculiar artistic genius which assimilates these Celtic
qualities.

> To distinguish at a glance, and apply the fitting word and phrase,
> to penetrate beneath the surface to the core of the apparent, to
> discriminate between gold and gilt, between natural gifts and
> acquired knowledge, to judge without waiting to ponder over
> bulky tomes for months or years, until the mind has dissipated
> the force of the first impression, to go straight, as if by magic,

to the inner meaning, and clutch at the very heart of the usurping mediocrity—these things Chateaubriand did, and these things have made him immortal (32).

Chateaubriand had died twenty-one years before Grierson first went to France, but in his work Grierson saw the inspiration for a revival of mysticism, philosophic idealism, organicism in language and art, and stern patience in social and political aspiration. In *The Celtic Temperament* Grierson set forth the shape this revival would take. "Out of the West [of France]," he wrote, "come the sound and the symbols of a great revival. A knell has been tolled for the old order of apathy and prejudice; the new dispensation will conciliate national animosities, and offer compensation to the genius and the language of an almost forgotten people" (43). Grierson thought the Celt to be an uncanny visionary who, as artist, possessed both spontaneous and profound insight to effect a new world outlook.

Victor Hugo was another French writer in whom Grierson saw this same inclination toward esthetic mysticism. He declared that Hugo was like a brilliant meteor which has "flashed across the horizon of modern progress."[19] Just what there was about Hugo which justified these panegyrics Grierson found adequately represented in Hugo's imagination, mysticism, intuitive genius, and all those qualities common to Grierson's ideal of poet-philosopher. Though exiled with the return of Louis-Napoleon Bonaparte, Victor Hugo represented for Grierson someone who sought the ineffable and who, according to George Lemaitre, felt "a spontaneous curiosity concerning the mysterious forces lying behind the forms and appearances of everyday life."[20] With such inward intensity as to affect his health, Hugo had brooded over occult doctrines for years; he was convinced that he had been selected to communicate with the Great Beyond.

All this mysticism attracted Grierson as much as did that of the elder Alexandre Dumas. In *Parisian Portraits* Grierson wrote that Dumas had told him in 1869, " 'Je crois au magnetisme' " (16-17)—adequate confirmation for Grierson that Dumas was to be taken seriously as one of France's great writers. If Grierson had needed further evidence, he could have cited Dumas' interest in palmistry, second sight, and trances.

The French writer most puzzling to Grierson was Mallarmé whom Grierson respectfully acknowledged as the chief aristocrat among the Symbolists. Yet Grierson neither fully accepted nor understood his artistic innovations. It was enough that in some way Mallarmé's words had an incantatory power of magic to transmit reality, though Grierson was largely unaware of Mallarmé's spiritual anxiety about the nature of reality. Again, it was sufficient that Mallarmé's salon was like a "cool mountain-spring" to a weary traveler whose "body rested while the spirit was being refreshed" (*Parisian Portraits*, 85, 87). Grierson was content to see Mallarmé stand by the fireplace and drone in his low tones, especially when his reflections aroused in his listeners a nostalgia for the remote past, for a sense of verbal purity, and for a mystical absolute.

In Grierson's sketch of Mallarmé and in a gracefully drawn vignette of Paul Verlaine, he inclined much more toward reminiscence than literary criticism. He savored his memory of Mallarmé's Tuesday evening gatherings when no one pressed the host to speak; the occasions were rather so many lessons in the virtue of silence. And in his memories of first meeting Verlaine at a sidewalk café, Grierson recalled the poet's "drone-dreamy eyes" and his dim meditations too subtle for words. Seeing Verlaine on later occasions in his comfortless attic apartment, Grierson compared him to "a bird of passage on a withered tree in the wilderness of Paris" (50). The quiet leadership of Mallarmé and the melancholy of Verlaine—whose two lines, "Il pleut sur le tolt / Et il pleur dans mon coeur," Grierson considered richer in human feeling than anything in the whole of Milton's *Paradise Lost*—mirrored something of Grierson's own dreamy self-image.

A brief summary of Grierson's critical judgments about French literature calls attention to an unflagging attack upon Realism and a constant sympathy with those individual writers whose works carried an unmistakably mystical tone. In these views Grierson seldom wavered. He wrote only occasionally about American authors. Except for Abraham Lincoln, who was his chief interest among all Americans, only Emerson, Whitman, and Mark Twain received more than passing remarks, and of these writers only Emerson was the subject of an entire essay.

Though Grierson was drawn to Emerson, one important reservation kept him from fully accepting the Concord poet-philosopher. Grierson was disturbed by what seemed to be Emerson's excessive intellectuality. He claimed, for instance, that Emerson had never known "real life," and that his "intellectual aloofness," his sophisticated Unitarianism, his loss of wonder, and, in short, his intellectuality, kept him short of genius.[21] Grierson knew little about Emerson's personal tragedies, nor did he understand the emotional complexities from which Emerson's intellectual life developed. Grierson's analysis is grossly superficial; yet it must be said that he was not writing literary criticism. He was attempting to capture a certain tone in Emerson and from it to generalize about the man. What he essentially saw in Emerson's writing was an excessive dialectic, itself inferring a complexity in subject matter which, to Grierson's way of thinking, might better have been distilled into shorter, more impressionistic essays. Lacking in Emerson was the aura of evanescence, a dimly mysterious tone which Grierson considered in no way incompatible with an aphoristic style. By contrast, he praised Walt Whitman, not for this kind of shadowy mysticism but rather for his flashing spontaneity, his essential simplicity, and his optimism. No evidence shows that Grierson had studied the several editions of *Leaves of Grass* revealing intricate prosody or that he had read Whitman's post-Civil War prose with its tone of disenchantment.

Grierson's few words on Mark Twain in *The Humour of the Underman* are to the point: "Mark Twain is so little of a poet that only once in his most serious book, *Life on the Mississippi,* does he speak adequately of the great river, and then only in ten lines" (114). Another cannonade, this one in *The Invincible Alliance,* annihilates him altogether: "The American humorist never cared to be an expert in anything but the dangerous science of piloting boats full of passengers on the Mississippi" (164).

These critical opinions are unacceptable today. During his own day, however, far more notable authorities were saying much the same thing, especially about Mark Twain, if indeed they were paying attention to him at all. In his *A Literary History of America* (1900) Barrett Wendell overlooks nearly everyone outside the New England tradition, and George E. Woodberry in *America in Literature* (1903) completely fails to recognize Mark Twain's achievement. Inadequate though it was, Ludwig Lewisohn's judgment of Emerson in *Expression in America* (1932) called attention to the same lack of emotional energy which Grierson had found wanting in the Concord writer. Three decades earlier Grierson had written in *The Celtic Temperament* that "A few of Omar's perennial roses, and a little of his wine, would have given colour and fragrance to [Emerson's] garden and some passion to his prose" (94)—the same qualities which would have enhanced Grierson's own essays. As for Grierson's enthusiasm for Whitman, it preceded by nearly a decade that of John Macy in *The Spirit of American Literature* (1908), generally held as a pioneering contribution to critical liberalism in American literature.

CHAPTER 7

The Valley of Shadows

I *Grierson's chef d'oeuvre*

GRIERSON'S MAJOR BOOK is *The Valley of Shadows,* "not a novel," he stated in his Preface, "but recollections of scenes and episodes of my early life in Illinois and Missouri" (v).[1] He said that ten years and all his fortune were required to write it, a statement difficult to verify except by the fact that he virtually ceased to publish anything during the six years immediately preceding 1909 and that he was, as Van Wyck Brooks said, alone in the depths of London. It was a book, according to Grierson, that culminated "a study [of Lincoln] which . . . required a period of thirty years."[2] In praising it, reviewers agreed it surpassed his previous volumes. In his introduction to the fifth edition (1948), Theodore Spencer called it "a minor classic" (xviii); Bernard DeVoto, in his Editor's Note to the same edition, deleted Spencer's adjective (ix). On the one hundredth anniversary of Grierson's birthday, Edmund Wilson wrote in his lengthy review for *The New Yorker* that the book must "be taken seriously as literature."[3] Reviewing the fifth edition for the New York *Times,* Lloyd Lewis asserted that "this haunting book deserved revival long ago."[4] Without question it stands as Grierson's major book and his chief claim to literary importance.

Long before writing it, he had left the prairies of Illinois. First in such cities as St. Louis, Chicago, New York, and Boston, then in Paris, Vienna, St. Petersburg, and London, he had had ample opportunity to shake the prairie dust from his shoes. Dining with royalty and artists in European courts and salons, he had left far behind his first home, a log house in Sangamon County, and the simple, unlettered prairie folk who were his neighbors. First as a musician, then as an essayist, he put aside his memory of the rustic dialects and anecdotes of the American pioneers. Attending to the social, philosophic, and literary goings-on in Europe and to a lesser degree in America, he wrote his essays as if he were totally unaware of the narrative possibilities of his early years spent in the Middle West just prior to the most important event in nineteenth-century American history. It is a striking spectacle in our literary history to see the essayist and cosmopolite return in imagination to the scenes of his childhood and to find there the material for his most impressive work.

In retelling those prairie years Grierson reminisced upon his past in order to capture what he wanted to bring into the present. His intention, more explicitly, was to depict the "silences" that belonged to the Illinois prairies and to create an atmosphere "which nothing but the term 'mystical' will fittingly describe" (1). In writing this book Grierson brought to a climax his case against the contemporary scientific and materialistic age. In other words, he wanted to make relevant to the present all the spiritual uniqueness he discerned in the past when, for example, he remembered that in Lincoln's reply to Stephen A. Douglas at the Alton debate "something issued forth, elemental and mystical" (198). Even though *The Valley of Shadows* is auto-biographically and historically important, the book's first importance to a person studying the life and thought of Grierson is its synthesis of his central ideas: that an old order has been replaced by a vulgar and materialistic democracy; that a new era of mystical art is slowly being born; that ultimate truth is spiritual; and that intuition and feeling lead to this truth.

The Valley of Shadows presents the *ante-bellum* days in the Middle West before the towns and railroads ended the old order and before the industrial West changed the Mississippi River into a commercial thoroughfare lined with smokestacks—a river described by T. S. Eliot in the *Four Quartets* as "unhonoured, unpropitiated by worshippers of the machine." Grierson attempted to interpret the moods of pioneers who sang about a new Canaan beyond the valley of shadows, who felt that the rush of events concerning slavery would lead to war, and who puzzled over the prophecies of their prairie seers whose peculiar acuteness to signs and symbols—to a comet or to a prairie fire—gave mystical importance to their divinations that someone from among them would rise to lead the people. Yet, for all its atmosphere, the book primarily stands as Grierson's most successful statement in a new century of scepticism of his indestructible faith in the reality of order, beauty, purpose, and spirit.

II *Readers' Appraisals*

The critical attention given the book in 1909 and shortly there-after indicated that, for its time, it was "a remarkable book, written by a remarkable man."[5] In a decade which in England greeted such non-Romantic works as *The Way of all Flesh* (1903), *Major Barbara* (1905), *The Man of Property* (1906), and *The Old Wives' Tale* (1908), and which in America saw the publication of *The Shame of the Cities* (1904), *The Jungle* (1906), *The Education of Henry Adams* (privately printed in 1907), and *Twenty Years at Hull House* (1910)—in short, in a decade of Realism and of increasing social and political com-plexity there appeared this book which, anachronistically, aimed at depicting "silences." At the outset Grierson stated the frankly Romantic approach and set the terms in which the book was to be read. Silences, mysticism, impulses, an all-inclusive noumena were to give the book its form. As outdated as such terms were in the new century, reviewers were disinclined to ignore Grier-son whose art, said one critic, may lack "startling reality" but should "not be quarreled with."[6] "I am disposed," said A. R. Orage, "to give him credit for one of the rarest qualities in literature, namely, atmosphere."[7]

Consistent with his own theory of esthetics, Grierson wanted to create impressions, not to write factual history. He stated in 1918 that his intention had been to depict "the spiritual atmos-phere of the Lincoln country in Lincoln's time—the atmosphere in which he lived and moved, thought and worked."[8] Recognizing this quality, critics repeatedly described this atmosphere as "poetic," "haunting," "uncanny," "drenched in mysticism."[9] From the conservative statement in the New York *Times* ("It is no ordinary book that Francis Grierson has written"[10]) to the exaltation of Shaemas O'Sheel (the book is "unsurpassed by anything since Homer and Xenophon"[11]) critics continually acknowledged Grierson's success in capturing the excitement in the prairie states prior to the Civil War. Mary Austin, who had spent her childhood in Illinois, was still another reader struck by the book's tonal authenticity. "Often while I have read your book," she wrote to him from London, "I would lay it aside and weep quietly for I knew not what.... It was as if something—the spirit of the land perhaps—which I had worshiped afar off, had turned back after all these years and hailed me."[12]

The historian Allan Nevins, also impressed by this strange atmosphere, gave more attention to the book's "great literary charm" than to its historical value.[13] Yet other readers called attention to Grierson's success as a chronicler of mid-nineteenth-century America. The New York *Times* stated outright that, "if there exists anywhere a work which paints so graphically and vividly the Lincoln country in Lincoln's time, it is unknown to us."[14] Bernard DeVoto in his Note to the fifth edition called it a book which goes to "the core of the American heartland." Samuel Eliot Morison and Henry Steele Commager went so far as to classify Grierson as a Realist and to place him in the unlikely company of Joseph Kirkland, Edward Eggleston, and E. W. Howe.[15] So successful was Grierson in portraying rural Illinois and its central figure, Abraham Lincoln, that Roy P. Basler considered the book, as one treating Lincoln, second only to Winston Churchill's *The Crisis* (1901) and, as an interpretation of Lincoln the mystic, "by far the most entrancing of any."[16] DeVoto, who was puzzled that Carl Sandburg should have overlooked the book, unaccountably erred; for Sandburg quoted extensively from it.[17]

Still another distinction given the book was its vivid autobiographical record of the author's childhood. What especially attracted the readers was the portrait of this astonishingly sensitive boy. Grierson had written, for example, that on one particular night during his childhood, he had motionlessly stood gazing at the sky: "The August splendour of the heavens, the atmosphere, palpitating with the presence of the All-ruling Spirit, diffused a feeling of an inscrutable power reaching out from the starry depths, enveloping the whole world in mystery" (64).

On another occasion the Mississippi River at dusk gave the boy "a *frisson* of the supernatural" and left him "thinking and wondering" (189). The impression given by passages such as these is of an unusually clairvoyant boy who knew that the pioneers understood and would follow the mystic genius of Lincoln because they too lived amid the prairie silences which gave to Lincoln his serene self-confidence, dignity, and gift of prophecy. In *The Valley of Shadows* Grierson appears as one who, even as a boy, shared in the understanding of nature's mysteries and of Lincoln's haunting power. Critics were not inclined to discount this self-portrait. They were fascinated by young Grierson. Surrendering to the author's intentions, one reviewer hailed

Grierson as one who, "young as he was ... divined vaguely the coming clash between slavery and abolition."[18]

In his Editor's Note to the fifth edition, DeVoto overstated the case that *The Valley of Shadows* "left no mark" following its publication in 1909; but his point has some validity. Grierson's book failed to make a sustained impression. Its readers praised it, then forgot it. Why this should have happened, in light of the book's initial reception, puzzled DeVoto who admired its "direct-ness" and "steadiness of perception" and its relevance to "the most momentous years of our history" (xi). The fact remains that no references to this book are made in the standard surveys of American literature.

DeVoto explained that the book failed to make an impact because in 1909 it had little if any vital meaning for its audience. He predicted that its fifth edition would at last make its mark:

> The hope is that it will now find its audience and that an American classic will be recognized for what it is. We are better prepared to appreciate it in 1948 than people were in 1909. Twice since then our hearts have been sifted out before the judgment seat. Twice we have lived through the oncoming of a great war. Twice we have lived in a trance of doubt and foreboding, feeling time carry us on toward the dark event which we seemed unable either to understand or to affect—till out of blindness and paralysis of the will we came to resolution, under-standing, and action (xi-xii).

In his 1948 review for *The New Yorker* Edmund Wilson was no less hopeful about the book's future, though his account of its initial reception and, more specifically, of Grierson's lost reputa-tion lacked something of DeVoto's deep stirrings. Wilson ex-plained Grierson's forgotten name by merely linking him with such "third-rate" writers of the day as Henry Van Dyke, F. Hopkinson Smith, James Lane Allen, and Thomas Nelson Page. This cursory explanation he deleted in his *Patriotic Gore* section on Grierson. This time he kept the question open, saying only that this "unique" book which had been "so strangely disregarded by historians and by writers on American literature," fills a "niche ... [he quotes DeVoto] which no other book quite fills."[19] He probed no further into the question of Grierson's faded name. However, the fact that he picked up Grierson again for extended treatment in *Patriotic Gore* indicates his conviction, stated in his 1948 review, that to go back among these "third-rate" figures is to unearth "some remarkable writers and some admirable books." "One of the very queerest of these queer cases," said Wilson, is Francis Grierson.

Clearly, a new appraisal of *The Valley of Shadows* needs to relate the book to Grierson's major ideas and to assess its literary qualities.

III A *Re-appraisal*

Anticipating that readers would object to the apparent lack of structure, Grierson explicitly stated in his opening sentence of the Preface that the book was not intended as a novel but only as "recollections of scenes and episodes" of his early years. Yet readers pointed out Grierson's departure from even his autobiographical intentions. They could not explain why he devoted three chapters (XXX-XXXIV) to General Frémont's western expedition in 1848; two chapters (XIII-XIV) to the love triangle of Hank Cutler, Vicky Roberts, and Jack Stone; and single chapters to General B. H. Grierson's raid through the South (XXV) and to General Grant's attack upon Vicksburg (XXVI). Since the setting of the first twelve chapters is Sangamon County, the time around 1858, and the main characters the Middle Border pioneers including Grierson's family, readers asked why the author digressed so freely in the latter part of the book.[20]

The thread of incident running through the book is not entirely broken even at the points where Grierson is most digressive. Rather than suspend the unity, he skillfully relates himself to each episode. For example, he describes the Frémont expedition as it was told to him by the general's old friends who occasionally came to his St. Louis headquarters where young Grierson served as Frémont's page. He tells the story of Hank Cutler, Vicky Roberts, and Jack Stone—among the first settlers in Sangamon County—as it was told to him one evening by a stranger who called at his family's cabin.[21] In the account of General Grierson's raid, the author states that he had known as a boy many of the men in the general's brigade. Finally, the chapter dealing with General Grant's Vicksburg attack in the spring of 1863 consists largely of the author's firsthand account of the army's mobilization around St. Louis during the preceding autumn. Even in these digressive chapters Grierson is close at hand.

The larger unity is in Grierson's artistic use of Sangamon

County which resembles, at least in function, William Faulkner's mythical Yoknapatawpha County. Both writers have made their respective regions microcosmic, and both have shown, to use Grierson's words, that "the old order passeth." Grierson then uses two additional key terms, thoroughly religious in their connotations. The first is the "valley of shadows," the changing and beclouded land in which his simple folk toil. The other is "a new Canaan" toward which they look and hope. With these three symbolic terms he succeeds in unifying the book in its larger scope, while also creating a tone consistent with the actions of his characters.

Central in Grierson's conception of "the old order" is his garden symbol. In the book's opening paragraph he descriptively surrounds the meetinghouse (where Azariah James, the preacher, will soon remind the congregation of the imminent valley of shadows) with all the beauty of the mythical Garden. On this "wonderful" Sunday morning "the flowers [were] in bloom, and the birds perched on the tallest woods were pouring forth their song! The fleckless sky, and soft, genial atmosphere had made of the desolate little meeting-house and its surroundings a place that resembled a second Garden of Eden" (5). With the symbol clearly drawn, Grierson contemplates the origin of the garden. Much like Thoreau who told in *Walden* of an "original proprietor" who reportedly dug Walden Pond and "an elderly dame" whose herb garden testified to her unequaled fertility, Grierson suggests an original proprietorship by imagining a woman and her husband long ago occupying his childhood home, a log house, a kind of Miltonic bower around which "sweet-william grew in great high bunches, interlaced with the branches of other shrubs" (33). He describes the luxuriance of the bower, not disfigured with "walks made by measure and strewn with sand and shells," but enchanted with the wild, free-growing flowers which in their indescribable color seemed to have "absorbed all the amaranth of a cloudless night, the aureole of early morning, and a something... that belongs to dreams and distance wafted on waves of colour from far-away places" (35). Chief among the flowers was the morning-glory, its vines arching the north door of the cabin and its blooms "revealing something in the kingdom of flowers" more beautiful than the Oriental elegance of the mantle "worn by the Queen of Sheba or by Solomon when he received her" (34). On one occasion, he remembered, the night sky illuminated the prairie in front of the cabin, so that the atmosphere "vibrated" with a strangely supernatural glow and the earth itself seemed to be "moving towards the stars." "The sky," he said, resembled "a phantasmagoria seen from the summit of some far and fabulous Eden" (63).

Sangamon County represents for Grierson the mythical Garden of Eden inhabited by the progeny of the original proprietors. Suggesting the ubiquitously spiritual presence of this progeny is the homely symbol of a rag-carpet covering the floor of the family's cabin. The cloth in the rug belonged to garments once worn by former occupants. Now covering the floor, these strips of cloth animate the whole house by representing in all their colors the sum of human experience. The rag-carpet, upon which daily prayers were said, is a reminder of the religious aspirations of all the occupants past and present, and serves as a symbol of human existence itself.

The entire garden, representing ideal nature, is alive with mystery, its every vagary carrying metaphysical import. The inhabitants perceive cosmic meaning in each vibrant event of nature; they transform all the occult messages, all the natural hieroglyphics, into strange prophecies pointing to the vital forces at work in shaping both a country and a race of men. These mystics, as they appear in *The Valley of Shadows*, stand for Grierson's idealization of the people who inhabit the garden, who live in the old order, but who also prophesy change near at hand. The rag-carpet is their ancestral ledger, the strips of saffron evoking "the presence of Kezia Jordan, and the darker hued memories of the Load-Bearer, Socrates, and Minerva Wagner" (39).

As Cooper said of his epical Natty Bumppo in the Preface to the Leatherstocking Tales, these heroic pioneers possessed "little of civilization but its highest principles as they are exhibited in the uneducated." In portraiture, old Minerva Wagner stands "facing the inexorable present" (51); Socrates is alone a "sufficient guarantee of his ability to take care of himself" (42); Elihu Gest, called the Load-Bearer, is a "veritable sphinx of the prairie" (21). Kezia Jordan, by conquering "the world of silences," has arrived at that level of existence when religion is not a thing of reason but "a state of perpetual feeling" (49, 50). Grierson wonders whether she knows better than anyone else the origin of the garden and the special meaning of the rag-carpet. He tells that when she once visited the log house the moments passed as if there were no clock ticking the time away and no regrets for the old days that would never return; and when at last Mrs. Jordan rose from her seat she looked more slender than ever in her simple dress of copperas-coloured jean; and when the clouds parted and the setting sun shone full on the windows, her spare figure cast a shadow that fell across the rag-carpet, and there, under her feet, were strips of coloured cloth, the counterpart of her own dress, and it seemed as if she had always belonged to the Log-House and ought never to leave it (52).

One other character—more sublime and mysterious than all the rest—who makes but one direct appearance, yet who fulfills the requirements of protagonist, is Abraham Lincoln. His influence is felt more strongly than that of any other character. From the time in the meetinghouse when Azariah James calls him the divinely appointed savior of America, he is the subject of all important conversation. Like an unseen guest, he looms in the background as a divine voice and becomes even more effective in portent than in person when he faces Douglas in a later chapter.

In all this idealization of the old order Grierson can be charged with overlooking in his Illinois garden such actualities as the pioneers' difficulties with storms, fencing, heavy sod, gophers, prairie chickens, and transportation prices; and, among the pioneers themselves, ignorance, greed, superstition, and illiteracy. Inviting as these matters were to the local-color Realists, Grierson had a much different purpose in mind. He was convinced of "something biblical" applied to the circumstances of the hour. He, therefore, transformed the pioneers, whom many historians have depicted as unlettered bumpkins,[22] into mystics, dreamers, and prophets. In the garden of Sangamon County these people are seen as linked in their primal work with destiny itself.

By the 1850's the old order had begun to pass and the real pioneering days in Illinois were nearing an end. The one-room log cabin was giving way to the frame dwelling of one, two, or more rooms. The "diamond plow" and horses were replacing ox teams and the hoe, and fences were enclosing the prairies. *The Valley of Shadows* is Grierson's testimony of affection for the old order and a sober acceptance of the new. With sadness he noted the passing of pioneers like Elihu Gest and Socrates whose quiet stoicism, eccentricities, and dialect reflected a certain pride which democracy was slowly eradicating in men. He saw that commodious homes were taking the place of the log houses, primitive woods, and wild flowers. Most unfortunate of all was that the Mississippi, which had flowed for ages "from the slumbering solitude of Minnesota," had now become the artery for "the shriek of iron whistles, the swirl of puffing machinery" (268).

But the chief symbol of the new order is neither the steamboat nor the deracinated or "successful" homesteader. Instead, the symbol is the "valley of shadows," darkened by the threatening clouds of civil war. Had Grierson gone farther back than the 1850's, he would have erred in supposing that the slavery question was a menacing cloud. Not until 1854 when Congress repealed the Missouri Compromise of 1820 did the angry passions of anti-slavery and pro-slavery groups decisively flare up. However, by the time of Grierson's setting in *The Valley of Shadows*, slavery and freedom had unquestionably become the main issues of the time.

He was, therefore, justified in darkening his scenes with the foreboding clouds of war, but his details are not always accurate. For example, he gives a false impression in showing that Illinois had a decided majority of abolitionists, only a small number of Know-Nothings or nativists, and an unimportant minority of rowdy anti-abolitionists. The majority of Illinois people were not abolitionists, as Lincoln himself at this time was not.[23] Abolitionists, eighty-five per cent of whose leaders were in New England,[24] were looked upon with as much disfavor in the Middle West as were the extremely aggressive, pro-slavery Southerners, who proposed after the Dred Scott decision to carry slavery into any state of the Union. In the northern part of Illinois were the settlers of predominantly Yankee stock who opposed slavery on principle; but the southern part of the state, which had drawn many of its settlers from the South, supported slavery. The testing ground was the central region of the state around Springfield. In 1858 when Lincoln opposed Douglas for election as United States Senator, the Republican Party was only four years old, and while it was strong in northern Illinois, it lacked decisive support in the "Egyptian" counties to the south. Grierson is not correct in showing a Lincoln majority, for the fact is that in the election of 1858 Douglas carried the state.

Grierson was, however, concerned less with historic fact than with atmosphere. In a characteristic way it is old Socrates who defines the issue of the oncoming war: "'I tell you what it is, if thar's ever goin' to be war it'll be betwix' them thet wants the land fer nothin' [letting 'the niggers do all the work'] an them thet wants it fer sunthin'" (45). From this point Grierson intensifies the feeling of impending crisis as Elihu Gest describes another set of polarities, this one between Douglas and Lincoln. "'The Jedge,'" as he opposed Lincoln in debate, "'looked like he war speakin' agin time, but Abe Lincoln looked plumb through the meetin' into the Everlastin'—the way Moses must hev looked when he see Canaan ahead—en I kin tell ye I never did see a man look thet a-way'" (67).

When the runaway slaves appear, the atmosphere is electric. Dominating the scene now is the Load-Bearer whose face showed "the inflexible will, the inexorable determination to dare and do" (93). The excitement of the next incident builds swiftly, as Grierson's father some distance away tries unsuccessfully to delay the pursuing slave hunters. To the Load-Bearer's cabin, which serves as a station on the Underground Railway now sheltering the runaways, comes another group of men and women, risking pursuit and injury at the hands of the slave hunters:

> There was the grey-bearded Squire Higgins, with his brows and kindly face; there was Cornelia Gest, slender, frail, and shrunken, in her seat; there was Azariah James, whose broodings defied all divination; there was Isaac Snedeker, stern and restless as an eagle about to take wing; and Martha Higgins, whose high massive forehead and arching nose contrasted strongly with the bountiful kindness of her dreamy eyes, while her smile expressed a faith that was infinite and undying (128).

Suddenly an immense glow lights the sky. A prairie fire, started as by magic, sweeps through the tall grass to within a quarter of a mile of the huddling, moaning slaves and their guardians. At the creek's edge the conflagration goes no farther, but it has left behind the charred ruins of Lem Stephens' house where the pursuing hunters had gathered. The Load-Bearer mysteriously warns, "'Thar's a mighty power movin' over the yearth; I ain't see a night sech ez this sence the comet fust appeared.... But thar's sunthin' else besides the wind thet's blowin' them flames, Squar Higgins" (129-30). The slaves begin to sing quietly, "To Canaan's fair and happy land / Where my possessions lie," while the Load-Bearer, their Moses, quietly hustles them into his wagon and leaves for the next station on their way north.

Grierson relaxes the tension of his episodic narrative for only a moment at the beginning of the next scene, "The Camp-Meeting," where a throng of people had come to receive the fire of God. For three days the evangelist tries in vain to ignite a spiritual revival among the frontiersmen who, instead, only loaf about. Then on the evening of the fourth day a storm strikes the camp. In a profusion of images, Grierson depicts a totally transformed Eden, now a "spectral" camp with its lanterns "swaying like grizzled phantoms on the brink of a yawning abyss" (149). Like a "fiery serpent" a lightning bolt streaks from the sky and splits an elm tree standing beside the platform. Amid the pealing thunder, great shouting arises. The revival is underway. The Load-Bearer cries above the lamentations, " 'You're hangin' to the hinges of Time by a hair!' " (150). Another voice calls out from "the shores of Tartarus."

Amid the wild uproar, someone suddenly discovers that Kezia Jordan's son lies dead beneath a portion of the fallen elm. Abruptly, an awful silence spreads through the meeting. Earlier, outside, Minerva Wagner's son had drowned as the result of drunken mischief. Both deaths are now seen as sacrificial events, omens of the conflict to come. Kezia Jordan, a Northerner, and Minerva Wagner, a broken Southerner, suffer the pain soon to be shared by thousands of other mothers. On this fateful note comes the climax of the book. It is a magnificently written chapter, the best in the book and certainly the only thing of its kind in American literature.

Grierson includes another portentous event, that of the historic comet which Giovanni B. Donati discovered on June 2, 1858. In an early reference to it Kezia Jordan says, " 'Thet comet's convicted a good many folks' " (23), and later in the book Grierson describes old Jordan, her husband, watching "the noiseless march of the comet" as it draws closer and closer to the earth (53). With each subsequent reference, the comet more fatefully signals the coming of war. Like Melville who called it "The meteor of the war" in his poem "The Portent, 1859," and like Sandburg who suggested that its appearance was hardly accidental,[25] Grierson interpreted it as part of the total apocalyptic drama.

He had ample precedent for this interpretation and for the Load-Bearer's prophecy, " 'jedgment ain't far off' " (153). The Middle West pulsated with religious fervor prior to the Civil War.[26] Lincoln himself frequently saw the war in the light of a Christian battle between good and evil.[27] Certainly a political judgment day was close at hand. The fact that the Southerners made it perfectly clear as early as 1856 that they would secede if a purely Northern party elected John C. Frémont, its presidential candidate, intensified the presentiments of doom should Lincoln be elected in 1860.

With Lincoln's election, Grierson and many other myth-makers took him to be strangely chosen to lead the people through the valley of shadows. Forgetting that Lincoln's political opposition cumulatively collected nearly a million more popular votes, Grierson describes the crowds as strangely prophetic about Lincoln's victory. They looked upon him as one who grew up among them, who by destiny rose to political prominence the same year Donati's comet appeared, who recognized all the apocalyptic portents, and, finally, who thought himself divinely appointed. The Lincoln whom Grierson pictured was a composite of a second Christ having "'such loads ez no man ever carried sence Christ walked in Israel'" (68) and of a second Moses looking "'the way Moses must hev looked when he see Canaan ahead'" (67).

It is as easy to correct the many false notions perpetuated by the legend as it is to recognize that Grierson is portraying a legendary Lincoln. That Lincoln was a politician before he was a statesman, and certainly before he was an oracle, is made clear by historians.[28] The notion that Lincoln was a giant among dwarfs disregards such brilliant men as William H. Seward, Edwin M. Stanton, and Salmon P. Chase. The legendary belief that Lincoln was an aloof and visionary seer who, in Grierson's words, "did not consult with others about what to say" (199), obscures the facts which show Lincoln acting with the tremendous forces of Congress and public opinion. Finally, as many historians have shown, the mythical account of Lincoln as the people's Moses omits the fact that the Republican Party was interested more in political strategy than in Lincoln's mystic genius; that his nomination was not effected until the third ballot; that at the news of the firing on Fort Sumter Lincoln's own region in southern Illinois immediately sympathized with the Confederacy; and that throughout the war nearly every segment of Northern opinion at times distrusted the President.[29] This whole legend is epitomized, in architecture, by the small log cabin, Lincoln's birthplace, which has been enclosed in a massive Greek temple at Hodgenville, Kentucky. Into its granite has been cut "an inscription which errs in the date of Lincoln's mother's birth, wrongly gives the names of her parents as Joseph and Nancy Shipley Hanks, incorrectly states that she was orphaned at the age of nine and reared by foster parents, and supplies false dates for Nancy's marriage to Thomas Lincoln and for their removal to Indiana."[30] These observations were made by Dixon Wecter who wryly added, "It seems a pity to carve so many misstatements, in a few lines, on so durable a medium as granite."

A more specific example can serve to illustrate Grierson's shaky grasp of facts as he drew his legendary Lincoln. He gives the impression that at the Alton debate Lincoln's statement of "the real issue" ("It is the eternal struggle between these two principles—right and wrong—throughout the world"[31]) was the "broadsider" that won the debate for him. Grierson states that "when Lincoln sat down Douglas made one last feeble attempt at an answer" (201). Actually Douglas' "feeble" reply ran to thirty-five hundred words; it was interrupted no less than forty-three times by applause and by such shouting as "Hurrah for Douglas," "Three cheers for Douglas," "Give it to him, he deserves it," "That's so," "That's the truth," "That's the idea, hurrah for Douglas."[32] Because the senatorship fell to Douglas, Lincoln could in fact claim no victory but a moral one.

In spite of its errors and false impressions, Grierson's account of this Alton debate is another remarkable section of *The Valley of Shadows*. Edmund Wilson called it "a strange and haunting description," and Carl Sandburg quoted large sections of it.[33] In it Grierson perpetuated the legend of Lincoln as prophet and savior. He showed him as the prototype of America's common man who possessed those qualities celebrated in the whole democratic dogma of the nation and given special definition in Whitman's Preface to *Leaves of Grass* (1855). Following Whitman's statement by fifty years, Grierson's image of Lincoln in *The Valley of Shadows* is the perfected common man, the towering individualist, the mystic genius, drawn from the legend which is still alive in America.

The "new Canaan"—the third of Grierson's chief symbols—lies beyond the valley of shadows. The phrase was on the lips of millions. To the Northern soldiers, "The Happy Land of Canaan" was a favorite song:

> The time of retribution am a-coming,
>   For with bayonet and shell
> We will give the rebels hell;
>   And they'll never see the Happy Land of Canaan.[34]

Easily parodying it to suit their own cause, the South added an ironic twist:

> It was on the 10th of June that the Yankees came to Bethel,
> They thought they would give us a trainin',
>   But we gave 'em such a beatin'
>   That they never stopped retreatin'
> Till they landed in the Happy Land of Canaan.[35]

In *The Valley of Shadows* the "new Canaan" represents not only the end of civil war but restoration of the garden, free from the curse of materialism in all its social, philosophical, and literary aspects. *The Valley of Shadows* is an allegory of a paradise lost and a vision of a paradise regained. Abraham Lincoln is the symbolic attestation of a new order of man. "What he stood for in the middle of the nineteenth century," Grierson declared in 1918, "the English-speaking people must stand for at the beginning of the twentieth."[36] The mysticism which the legend ascribed to both Lincoln and his age suggested to Grierson the instrument by which materialism could be overcome by a new spiritual authority. This is the theme of Grierson's final works after his return to the United States in 1913.

IV *Summation*

Among those persons who have read *The Valley of Shadows* there has been the tendency to overlook the book's weaknesses in favor of its uniqueness in Middle Border and Civil War literature.

In this book Grierson's main business, as he stated it, was "to depict the 'silences' that belonged to the prairies, for out of those silences came the voices of preacher and prophet and a host of workers and heroes in the great War of Secession" (v). These silences obviously meant much to the author, and it is his responsibility to make them compelling to the reader. To the extent that Grierson is recalling experiences and impressions which have a special and peculiarly personal meaning, he may be using a foreign language to the unpersuaded reader. Like that of any artist, his task is to put subjective feeling into language which elicits similar feelings from the reader. Throughout much of the book Grierson succeeds in doing this—with sweeping lyricism and power. Even so, his weakness comes, at this point, in his occasional failure to sustain a sensible image. When he seeks to communicate mystical silences and their occult meanings, he too often allows abstract generalizations to smother an otherwise sufficiently effective image.

Rather than describe concretely the objects evoking in him these feelings of supernatural immanence, he simply announces that there was a certain atmosphere. In the best tradition there is, of course, a legitimate place for abstraction. But Grierson shows his weakness when, fearing that the drama itself will not carry the feeling, he vitiates the presentation by resorting to magniloquent generalization. An example is the description of his mother's evening prayer: "The words, coming from that magical voice, unlocked the reservoirs of the infinite, and faith came rushing through the flood-gates" (36). Drenched in metaphysical abstractions, his next paragraph recounts that the pendulum of the family clock "went like a plummet to the depths of the soul," bringing forth "that part of Nature which is hidden from our sight by a thin veil behind which we can sometimes hear the voices on the other side." In other places, words like "infinite depths," "unearthly yearnings," "everlasting dreams," "silences," "soul" are stock-in-trade; they suggest a paucity of sensibility at those times when Grierson most wishes to persuade his readers about the voices he hears amid the silence.

One voice was that of the owl, described in a subsequent paragraph: "The first note had an *indescribable quality,* and the series of *half-veiled* trumpet calls that followed produced on me a *sensation never to be forgotten.* They sounded like *nothing else in Nature*" (38, italics mine). If the reader had previously known such an experience, his own recall would make Grierson's description easier to re-create imaginatively. But to the uninitiated, Edmund Wilson's assertion in 1948 is hardly convincing: "every word seems solid and every detail seems real . . . every sentence shows something of Flaubert's solicitous care"—a statement he re-phrases in 1962, asserting again that Grierson polished "every sentence with a solicitude that was almost Flaubertian."[37] Grierson's practice is much like one's fortifying wine with wood spirit. Many writers have done it. Passages in *The Valley of Shadows* vaguely remind one of *Childe Harold's Pilgrimage* where Byron had little to say and tried to compensate for lack of matter by manner. More particularity would not only have improved Grierson's style but would have convinced the reader that prairie silences contain all that Grierson insisted they did. It would have also reassured him that the author's occasional betrayal of unliterary sensibility ("the rose, the flower of fashion and convention, the one with least suggestive influence on the heart and the affections" [32]) is incidental to his greater skill with the concrete image.

Yet Grierson in this book is at his best. If from reading it a person fails to learn the secrets of prairie silences (Grierson soberly warned that "only the most clairvoyant minds can penetrate to the inner meanings of the book"[38]), he can still agree with Bernard DeVoto's opinion that "there is a niche in American literature for *The Valley of Shadows,* one which no other book quite fits." He added, without reservation: "It does superbly what no other does at all: it had no predecessors and will have no successors."[39]

CHAPTER 8

Last Years

I *The Jazz Age*

NEARLY TWENTY-FOUR YEARS had passed since Grierson had been in the United States. The threat of European war brought him back in 1913. Two years earlier he had written in *The Invincible Alliance* that the next war, far from being a "dress parade show," would be "a simple affair" of calculated famine and slaughter (18). In his frenetic warnings of what lay ahead, he stressed the danger of a German blockade and the consequences should it succeed in starving England. By 1913 he knew that only the slightest provocation would touch off the whole European powder keg. He sailed with Tonner on the *Lusitania*, arriving in New York on November 30, still the "strange fish" he had been in London. A New York *Evening Post* reporter sent to interview him wrote that Grierson's lips and cheeks were rouged, his eyes darkened: "His hair was arranged in careful disorder over his brow, his hands elaborately manicured and with many rings on his fingers; he wore a softly tinted, flowing cravat."[1]

Within two weeks Arthur Farwell, the editor of *Musical America*, welcomed him back as a "musical liberator."[2] Other articles appeared in quick succession, all calling attention to Grierson's remarkable career.[3] From these hosannas a small-scale Grierson cult developed. Claude Bragdon, author of numerous books on occultism, kept in close company with him. Edwin Björkman, who earlier the same year had published *Voices of To-Morrow* which placed Grierson with Maeterlinck and Bergson as rebels against materialism, enthusiastically reported on Grierson's musical recitals. Edwin Markham invited him to his home several times. Judge Ben Lindsey, an old acquaintance from Grierson's days in the West, introduced him to Henry Ford. Soon he was invited to membership in the National Press Club and the Chevy Chase Club.

During the first years after his return, he lectured and gave piano recitals up and down the East Coast and as far west as Wisconsin and Illinois where he appeared at the state universities. These public appearances, however, failed to support him financially. Tonner tried to assist by giving private French lessons in Washington, D. C. He also sought employment at the Bureau of Public Information, but even with the help that Herbert Hoover offered through letters of recommendation Tonner was unsuccessful. He was also turned down by the John Lane publishing offices in New York. By 1918 Tonner, now fifty-six years old, found it difficult to break into any new venture. Grierson, at seventy years of age, was feeling the strain of the lecture and recital circuit. Tired of the dull audiences he had to face, even more fatigued by the travel required, and depressed by waning publicity, Grierson wrote to Bragdon:

> The art in a thing no longer counts here; it is the person they want to see, and if the person does not possess high social connections in the old country so much the worse for that person. And it is futile to go against this awful snobbery. It pervades everything.... And you and myself, and others, will have to take the world on the basis of the blank and impudent materialism on which it rests, or we shall get little accomplished while we live. Therefore, be wise! A very *grande dame* here, and one with famous ancestors, advised Waldemar to address the fashionable audience at her mansion, before the recital, and tell the company who my ancestors were. Think of it! You see my art, my books, my poetry would not be enough![4]

Before Grierson moved to California, where he found more restful conditions, he published several of his American lectures as *Illusions and Realities of the War* (1918). In these essays Grierson reasserted the need for Anglo-American unity. He balefully described the enemy, Germany, as a nation which had lost its nobility, honor, and code of laws and which was now led by "lawless, freebooting desperadoes" (52). Giving way to near-hysteria, he called the Germans "monsters, brutes, cut-throats and the like"; decried the "namby-pamby" way American journalists treated the "diabolical" Teutons; and voiced his fear that, with such a large Teutonic population in New York, Chicago, St. Louis, Cincinnati, and Milwaukee, "all America was rapidly becoming Prussianised" (40). German materialism (here was Grierson's main indictment) bred "callous arrogance and a profound contempt for all that is lovable in human nature" (126); it was a corruption to the land, the sooner scourged the better. In short, Germany was a menace to mankind, an argument echoing that of Woodrow Wilson and countless Americans who found it the perfect justification for America's entry into the war. But, unlike Wilson and the Progressives, Grierson went on to insist that punishment continue to be severely pressed upon Germany, once defeated by Allied arms.

The Anglo-American unity which Grierson also advocated claimed its urgency on other grounds than mutual commercial expansion. Of more importance to him was the moral advantage which the alliance would establish. Ideological ties would make it possible for both countries to preserve the strength necessary to resist alien patterns of political, social, and religious thought. He argued that the Teutonic and Yellow races would not give up their ambitions to destroy English and American unity, to him a dreaded prospect which must be allayed by the two nations' dissolving their animosities toward each other. Grierson broadly favored that America's military alliance with England continue after the war when Germany's aim, he predicted, would once again be to control all Europe. He argued that this alliance could have its basis in the many common ideologies which America and England already shared. In this view Grierson sided with the conservatives in this country whom Robert La Follette and the Progressives continually attacked on the grounds that, in fact, America had few ideological ties with Britain's hereditary monarchy.

Illusions and Realities of the War reflects the mind of a political conservative, a racist, and an old man contentious in matters of foreign and domestic affairs. With waxed moustache and English proprieties, he believed that, unless traditional customs were promptly restored in America, this nation would sink into a moral chaos worse than the one which the Allied armies were out to correct in Germany. His reaction to the reckless and rowdy years after 1914 affords an affecting picture of an aging gentleman shocked by a young generation freed from all restraint. Eric Goldman's description of the New Poetry, New History, New Democracy, New Art, New Woman—"the new anything so long as it was new and gave an intoxicating sense of freedom"⁵—was the kind of nose-thumbing revelry Grierson found himself in the midst of. *Illusions and Realities of the War* registers Grierson's disgust at a nation given over to jazz and the "barbaric" saxophone; to dancing in a "syncopated embrace"; to cigarettes and gin, Jung and Freud; to sex and the true-confession magazine; to materialistic science; to pragmatism; to the cult of efficiency; and, in general, to what Harold Stearns described as America's "modern, Western, abundance-founded, this-world-ly, anti-mystical, gay and progress-convinced attitude."⁶

Grierson's opinions in this book fly helter-skelter. After long years in Europe he now found the American scene beyond anything at its worst that he had dreamed of. The "smart set" and their emotional craze he thought utterly repellent. "It matters very little," he declared, "what the thing is, what it stands for, so long as it is supposed to give a new shock to the nerves, a new vibration to the senses" (168-69). Whether it was rag-time, Cubism, or free verse, to Grierson it was loose and disjointed, "starting anyhow and ending anywhere" (156):

> It is a fungous growth and a negroid development, in which the primitive and barbaric mingle with singular unity and suggestiveness. Just as soon as it is realized that these new crazes and isms are un-American, and opposed to all phases of national and normal ideas of progress, just so soon will they be tabooed as unpatriotic, dangerous to the public welfare, and impossible. This rage, like others equally loose and decadent, does not tally with moral courage, physical fitness, and love of one's country (157-58).

In the foot-loose and raucous 1920's Grierson saw the death of all the causes he had fought to bolster. He especially regretted the end of novels and essays dealing with the supposedly higher aspirations of man. But the returning soldier, he said, would not be content with Pickwick or Monte Cristo after he had "waded in trench mud, breathed poisonous gas, staggered under the intonations of bombs hurled from modern howitzers" (69). Grierson faced the inevitability of a John Dos Passos and an E. E. Cummings, but he cared not a jot for their task.

He said in this same book that the only immediate hope for America's salvation was to be found in special reform movements such as prohibition. Interpreting this movement as a sign of a "spiritual" revolution and regeneration, he anticipated other reforms destined to follow the prohibition victory, "reforms so great that the drowsy East will hardly have time for a full realization of the facts" (177):

> The cabaret will pass out with the saloon. The next closeout will be the Sunday movies, and the next a limit fixed for all movies and a ban on the vice pictures. The churches will boycott the picture shows except where the subjects are of a highly moral and religious nature. Laws will be framed against loose plays, ribald songs, and vaudeville acts. All Sunday games and sports will cease.... Among the most drastic enactments will be a complete revision in the methods of teaching at the schools and universities. Agnosticism and materialism will be rudely thrust out and not permitted to take refuge in any other place, in any other visible form.... People will retire much earlier and rise much earlier, hence more work will be accomplished and the health of the nation will improve fifty per cent.... The rage for banquets will cease because drink was in many cases the prime factor in that mode of pleasure seeking. A ban will be placed on banquets that last after ten o'clock. After the manufacture of alcohol ceases scores of vicious elements will pass away of themselves (178-79).

Grierson concluded his bizarre vision of a new-born America: "After the closing up of the bars and saloons, with all they imply, and abolishing fifty other evils that beset humanity, we shall begin the great crusade of crusades—we shall pass laws for the abolishment of big cities. The cities must go, for until they pass all the schools, churches, and colleges in the world will not reform society or keep men and women from the down grade" (181).

Finding less and less in America that suited his taste, and himself growing more cantankerous all the while, Grierson was ready to terminate his role as rebel and critic that he had played obstinately for thirty years. He was weary of battling what he thought to be the psychic malady of the modern world. He was thoroughly repelled by the parvenus who, as J. K. Huysmans wrote in *A Rebours* (1884), had "instincts of gorillas." Even discontented with his own misshapen views of social reform, he finally cared little if the materialists went to hell. Buried like a husk in a new society, he succumbed to the lure of Spiritualism. This time he was not the shrewd practitioner of his San Diego days; rather, he was a quiet believer who surrendered to the claims of spiritual wisdom, the only solace for his general fatigue. Since the days of his young manhood, science in psychic research had intrigued him. One of his favorite theories had been that a spiritual reaction aided by science would ultimately follow a drastic material action. Now it offered the only hope. Reports of a "new movement" coming from the Far West interested him. Clearly, he was ready to go to what Van Wyck Brooks termed the "psychic belt"[7] of Southern California.

Before leaving the East Coast, Grierson published one more volume, a thin collection of pieces entitled *Abraham Lincoln, the Practical Mystic* which appeared in 1918. Though it took as its theme the same Lincoln legend developed in *The Valley of Shadows*, this new book about Lincoln had a special relevance to the day. Another great war had just ended, and Grierson, as before, hoped for a spiritual renaissance to sweep the land, a new mystical awareness, a "new birth"—as Lincoln himself had said. In this hope Grierson now drew the figure of a mystical Lincoln in bolder and more millennial outlines than he had done in 1909. He wanted Lincoln's strangely powerful mysticism to exemplify that quality of character which Grierson believed to be the only antidote to "the new pagan Kultur, which opposes not only Christian morals but everything that places the spiritual above the material" (13). In this volume, which serves as a kind of epilogue to *The Valley of Shadows,* Grierson echoes his own long protests against materialism; and he offers as its only effective counter-force those religious values which he thought accounted for Lincoln's triumph. Grierson envisioned a new mystical epoch, uniquely Anglo-American, which would accord with the old American Dream and with all its sublime principles enunciated by Lincoln. Holding to this view throughout the book, he concluded by proclaiming: "Amidst the strife of contending factions the thunder of upheaval reverberates from continent to continent, heralding the close of a dispensation that has known the trials and triumphs of nearly two thousand years, from which is emerging the mystical dawn of a new day" (93).

Reviewers hailed the book with mixed feelings.[8] The least generous critic called it a "bizarre and pathetically insipid volume, by one of our most distinguished 'culture-philistines.'" "We are told in so many words," he said, "to fall down upon our knees and worship Abraham Lincoln, 'the greatest practical mystic the world has known for nineteen hundred years.' One suspects that Mr. Grierson intends something very mystical here, but the secret is between him and Abraham Lincoln."[9] This review and others like it did not discourage him from seeking the certitudes proffered by Spiritualism. In 1919, his morale braced by his old friend Mary Austin who called him "wonderful,"[10] he decided to devote all his remaining energies to the Spiritualist cult. Celebrating his seventy-first birthday in Toronto, where he had gone to lecture on Theosophy prior to his long journey to Los Angeles, Grierson received a gold watch as a gift from his students and listeners who, in their note to him, expressed gratitude for his showing them "the Way to the Higher Life which is so comprehensive, marvellous and a Life filled with wonder."[11]

II *California, Spiritualism, Death*

Southern California after World War I attracted many well-known literary figures who, their careers nearly finished, wished for a restful place to spend their old age. Julian Hawthorne moved to Pasadena, Hamlin Garland went to Hollywood where he grew interested in Spiritualism, and Theodore Dreiser's strongest attraction to mysticism occurred when he settled in Southern California. Later in his career Upton Sinclair also moved there. Such foreign writers as Thomas Mann, Franz Werfel, and Aldous Huxley found California a suitable retreat, though some of them, including Huxley, could not resist satirizing it. Huxley's *After Many a Summer Dies the Swan* (1939), Evelyn Waugh's *The Loved One* (1948), and J. B. Priestley's *Midnight on the Desert* (1937) poke fun at California, a region further ridiculed by Frank Lloyd Wright as catching "all the commonplace people" whose Mecca—Los Angeles—is inhabited, said another observer, by "middle-aged obese women from somewhere in the Middle West, lying naked in the sun."[12]

When Grierson arrived in this city of novelties, quacks, realtors, and pathological optimists, the nation was undergoing a revolution not only of morals and manners but also of science. Einstein's theory of relativity had pointed to the inadequacy of classical mathematics and had implied the incompetence of both physics and mathematics to deal with a fundamentally irrational universe. To many persons the interpretation of the term "relativity" justified the denial of all absolutes. The extreme subjectivism which resulted from this theory, freeing persons from notions of fixed space and time, accounted for Claude Bragdon's query, "Are we on the point of discovering that the only reality is thought-consciousness?"[13]

P. D. Ouspensky carried subjectivism further by declaring in *Tertium Organum* (1920) that through the "higher conscious-ness" one can see beyond the three-dimensional world of spatial and limited objects. To many students Einstein's theory refuted materialism; Einstein, it was said, had shown that matter could be converted into nonmateriality (energy), an idea which gave impressive support to religious groups claiming that matter was immaterial or, according to Mary Baker Eddy's *Science and Health* (1875), that there is "no life, truth, intelligence, nor sub-stance in matter."[14] In an article entitled "The Latest Ideas in Physics" written for *Harper's Magazine* (April, 1924), Sir Oliver Lodge asserted that there is "more than a hint" that electrons "are essentially resolvable into ethereal energy." Alfred North Whitehead's Lowell Lectures published as *Science and the Modern World* (1925) stressed a philosophy of nature as organic rather than materialistic, as function rather than as entity.

The point to be made is that the subjective mind was seen as gaining dominion over matter, and that matter in its three-dimensional definition was to many thinkers an inadequate reality. It was not surprising that Jung in the early 1930's detected a new psychological interest among people to whom the outer world of matter offered nothing of the psychic life they sought. According to Jung in his *Modern Man in Search of a Soul*, this trend significantly explained the growth of Spiritualism and Theosophy. Gerald Heard in his study *These Hurrying Years* (1934) thought that the most important discovery of the 1920's was mental telepathy. To Frederick Hoffman, "the agony of a spiritual quest in a world that regarded spiritual matters with indifference was one of the most profound emotional experiences of the 1920's."[15]

However, as Hoffman points out, people in the 1920's who were turning to the psyche or to the fourth dimension of cosmic consciousness (Ouspensky's term) were pursuing science and knowledge—not religious faith. For example, Jung saw that the awesome discipline of science still gave the public a feeling of confidence, even though the findings of modern science had dispelled old Newtonian certainties. Science was not displaced by the New Thought movements in which Bragdon, Eddy, Ouspensky, and many others participated, nor was it set aside by Jungian or Freudian psychology. Instead, it was summoned to even greater challenges, its "monastic regimen," as Hoffman says, inspiring the public as a priest would have in an earlier day. In fact, many people thought that science and "higher consciousness," working hand in hand, would bring about the kind of spiritual renaissance which Grierson envisioned.

Long before Grierson went to Los Angeles in 1920, he had shown interest in the new role of science. In *The Celtic Temperament* he had written that science was "the most romantic and mystical thing in this matter-of-fact world" (xxii-xxiii). Throughout his career Grierson thought about the mystery of extrasensory or intuitional perception and the potentialities of a nonmaterial science to deal with it. Newly invented wireless telegraphy gave promise of a new medium for mental communication which, in turn, would confirm the possible control of invisible forces. Any previous doubts about scientific Spiritualism he now put aside, and for his new home he appropriately chose Los Angeles, the city of angels.

Invaded by a steady stream of newcomers, Los Angeles in the 1920's was the scene of a spectacular "religious" awakening. Religious fakers had their heyday. During the decade the epidemic spread to such proportions that legislation finally forced soothsayers, fortune tellers, and swamis to operate under license. Los Angeles was the oasis for students of divine healing, occult science, spiritual and mental phenomena, reincarnation, and astrological revelations. By 1926 the city had seven separate churches of the American Theosophical Society and twenty-one of the National Spiritualist Association.[16] Because of its many esoteric groups Los Angeles acquired the reputation, which it has not lost, of having an incomparable multiplicity and diversity of faiths.

In this sunny haven for any and all beliefs Grierson enjoyed congenial company among those who embraced the popular belief, simplified and systematized by scientific method, that the mind can achieve mastery over matter and that higher consciousness can subject space and time to its own dominion. Grierson's optimism was like that of Ouspensky who went so far as to declare in *Tertium Organum* that such consciousness of the cosmos would place the individual on a new plane of existence. It would, Ouspensky said, "make him almost a member of a new species."[17] Any cult claiming special authority to bless this "new species" Grierson felt sympathetic toward. Mrs. Annie Besant, successor to Madame Blavatsky as international head of the Theosophy Society, said in the New York *Times* (August 26, 1926) that such a species was presently being formed in the West, and she went to Ojai, California, in 1926 to supervise it personally in the name of Theosophy. At last, then, Grierson had found a haven where he could spend his final years and see, in Los Angeles, his hopes for America fulfilled.

It was the cult of Spiritualism with its emphasis upon the interpretation of messages from the dead which fascinated Grierson in Los Angeles. What seemed so promising to him was the use the cult was making of the new science of thought transmission, given impetus at the time by the inventions of telegraphs, telephones, and gramophones. Many persons supposed that, when Walt Whitman had written of "the body electric," he had discovered an order of reality as important to the understanding of the physical world as to the mental. The theory was enlarged to suggest that the human brain with its own chemical changes was a kind of radio transmitter sending out electrical vibrations. These currents or vibrations could then be picked up if an instrument were invented sensitive enough to detect them. Upton Sinclair's excitement in his book *Mental Radio* (1930) was as great as Thomas Edison's when he wished to solve the whole problem of thought transference "on a scientific basis, as chemistry is put, and [withdraw it] from the hands of the charlatan and the 'medium.' "[18] Edison proposed to build an apparatus, "a sort of valve," that would increase many times whatever original force lay behind it. "Now follow me carefully," he wrote in 1920:

I don't claim that our personalities pass on to another existence or sphere. I don't claim anything because I don't know anything about the subject. For that matter, no human being knows. But I do claim that it is possible to construct an apparatus which will be so delicate that if there are personalities in another existence or sphere who wish to get in touch with us in this existence or sphere, this apparatus will at least give them a better opportunity to express themselves than the other crude methods now purported to be the only means of communication with those who have passed out of this life. I merely state that I am giving the psychic investigators an apparatus which may help them in their work, just as optical experts have given the microscope to the medical world.[19]

After writing this account Edison did not refer to the "apparatus" again; his biographers fail to mention it at all. Nevertheless, it is clear that science and the mind interested him as much as many other contemporaries who associated mental phenomena with "vibrations" and "receiving sets." When, for example, Mrs. Besant spoke to a Chicago convention of the American Theosophical Society in 1926, the New York *Times* reported the event in the jargon of the cult:

> Mental "receiving sets" of theosophists attending the convention in Chicago are receiving "vibration messages" from all parts of the world, it was asserted by delegates. The minds of many cultivated thinkers among believers in theosophy have become attuned to thought vibrations from others and the "reception," although marred by earthly "static" is at least as good as that of early radio receiving sets, it was declared.[20]

Hamlin Garland boasted that his circle of mediums in Los Angeles had received messages from the spirits of Henry James, Sir Arthur Conan Doyle, Dwight L. Moody, and Walt Whitman. In her book *Open the Door* (1935) noted Spiritualist Edith Ellis recorded messages from even more illustrious persons: the Virgin Mary, Jesus Christ, Abraham Lincoln, and Madame Blavatsky.

Francis Grierson's contribution to Spiritualist literature was an eighty-two page book called *Psycho-Phone Messages* which he published privately in Los Angeles in 1921. In its introduction Tonner wrote that Grierson first used the word "psycho-phone" in his Toronto lectures in 1919, "a year before Thomas Edison announced his intention of devising an instrument which . . . will serve to establish intercourse between our world and the world of the spirit" (5). Long converted to Grierson's genius, Tonner said that this small book would appear to many readers "as the most interesting phase of Mr. Grierson's psychic gifts, for the seer who ushered in the new mystical movement by the publication of 'Modern Mysticism' in 1899 is now the recorder of messages which must induce thinking and unprejudiced minds to pause and consider such matters in a new light, and it is to be hoped that many more messages like these may be recorded by the same hand" (7-8). Grierson's own introductory statement emphasized that the "psycho-phonic waves" by which the messages were imparted "are as definite as those received by wireless methods" (15). He also explained that he was placing the reader "in communication with some of the most far-reaching minds of the past hundred and fifty years" (23).

With perhaps some static, though unreported by either Grierson or Tonner, the psycho-phone on September 7, 1920, went into action. Its initial recording was an unpleasant message from the spirit of Thomas B. Reed, late Speaker of the House of Representatives, whose first jarring sentence was: "The formidable imbecility of the Senate rivaled the fantastic irritability of the President" (21). The late Mr. Reed also heckled Woodrow Wilson for his naïveté at Versailles. Next was General Grant's message which reiterated the one sent by Reed, adding that the United States must fortify its southern borders as well as Panama against increasing numbers of foreign agents operating in Mexico and South America. Thomas Jefferson's spirit criticized the inability of both Republican and Democratic parties to cope with the cross-purposes of North and South. Elizabeth Cady Stanton continued her arguments of twenty-five years earlier on the subject of women's rights and, on this psycho-phonic day, of women's superior spirituality. Benjamin Franklin puzzled over Andrew Carnegie's motives in building libraries but in failing to buy books for them. John Marshall warned against Socialism; Daniel Webster echoed the warning against so-called bohemian Socialism. Oliver Wendell Holmes pleaded for common sense among the electorate, while Benjamin Wade (late governor of Ohio and also United States Senator) asked for "diplomatic tact and political judgment" among the elected. Lincoln predicted the failure of the League of Nations; Stephen A. Douglas warned that a war with England would "Russianize" the United States within three months. Henry Ward Beecher's testimonial vibrations, distinctly harmonious with Grierson's lectures in 1918, asked: "What is causing so much crime? Not one, but many elements of decadence, all operating together, among which I can name rag jazz, high balls, cabarets, free verse, neurotic art, sentimental optimists, cheap notions of progress, automobilism, lack of child discipline, absence of fear among people under the age of forty..." (72-73).

If one grants a seventy-three-year-old Los Angeles Spiritualist the privilege to correspond with spirits of the dead, one need not strain to convert him. Agnes Repplier could not resist the comment, however, that what was so annoying about "spirit authors" like Grierson was that they were beyond any show of diffidence as they proffered their counsel. Their didacticism, she observed, produced "volume after volume of 'messages'... bearing nothing of value."[21]

Certainly nothing is accomplished by dismissing Grierson as a hoax which, in fact, he was not. Except for his questionable dealings in San Diego with the High brothers, his career had been one of genuine achievement in both music and literature. As for his spiritualistic exercises—his spirit messages from the dead, his purported release from three-dimensional life—in all this, it is important to remember that Grierson was typical of many Americans whose serious concern over spiritual communication has not yet been fully studied. Spiritualism offered Grierson and many others like him a new possibility for existence. In Los Angeles Grierson intended no deception upon anyone, and he sought no proselytes for his own status. That there were those who did sincerely desire to free themselves from the incubus of materialism through revivalism, Spiritualism, Christian Science, and the New Thought is a fact not taken lightly by George Santayana who saw nothing incredible in a person's finding new channels for cosmic or inner energy not hitherto discovered.[22]

Personal loyalties shown by Grierson's friends vindicate claims against him of fakery. Waldemar Tonner's devotion was unquestionably steadfast. Van Wyck Brooks's letter of condolence written to Tonner a month after Grierson's death in May, 1927, best indicates the affection felt by those persons who knew both him and Tonner:

> Mr. Grierson's death must have been a very great shock to you, but it must be a great gratification to you to realize all that you did for him in loving devotion and unwearful kindness for so many years. I know how your own friends and Mr. Grierson's friends tell about that, how warmly they admire you for these years of unselfish service. I hope that all good luck may attend you in the future. Mr. Grierson's host of friends are all yours and they will all think of you with deep and warm sympathy as long as they remember him.[23]

Edwin Markham, Sara Teasdale, and Zona Gale valued their friendship with Grierson. Frank A. Miller, Master of the Mission Inn in Riverside, California, was on close terms with Grierson who on occasions gave piano recitals at the inn. The list of friends lengthens when one reads the felicific letters he received from persons whom he had invited to contribute to an anthology of poetry he was editing during the months prior to death. Witter Bynner, Mary Austin, Mark Van Doren, Shaemas O'Sheel, Edwin Arlington Robinson, and Lillian White Spencer were a few of those who wrote of their respect for him.

Of special interest is a person Grierson met following a recital in 1923. A Hungarian count, Michael Albert Teleki, introduced himself to Tonner and Grierson, and within a short time the friendship brought Tonner and Teleki together as partners in a dry cleaning business. Living in adjacent quarters, Tonner and Grierson stayed in close association with Count Teleki and his mother, Countess Rose Teleki, both of whom had fled as refugees from the family's castle of Gernyeszeg near Dumbravioara, Hungary, just after World War I. For a few years the modest income from the business and from Grierson's lectures on cosmic consciousness, four-dimensional space, and vision, and from interviews and lessons in poise, power, expression, and practical psychology provided adequate income for Grierson, Tonner, and the two Telekis. During these last years Grierson remained in good health, though he was bothered by gout to the extent of having to wear special shoes which were sliced along the sides and opened at the toe.

Unfortunately Grierson could no longer interest publishers in his writing. The John Lane Company which had already published four of his books showed no interest in *Psycho-Phone Messages*, which Grierson finally brought out at his own expense. He and Tonner were also unsuccessful in finding anyone to publish the anthology of poetry Grierson had edited. Mary Austin wrote to Tonner that he should "not be discouraged if one or a half dozen publishers refused it."[24] After Grierson's death, however, Tonner abandoned the project. He then tried without success to persuade someone to publish Grierson's memoirs, *Anecdotes and Episodes*, which in 1925 both he and Grierson had shown to various people. In 1929 Claude Bragdon showed the manuscript, still unpublished, to Alfred A. Knopf who read it with interest but did not take it. A New York agent, John

Clapp, tried unsuccessfully to peddle it. "Everybody says it is *rare* and *rich*," he wrote to Tonner, "but all recognize that the people who buy books don't *know* Grierson. The one chance is to find a gifted writer who will take up *Grierson himself*—his life and works—and make a real book about him in which the auto-biography may be *set*."[25] He suggested that Carl Van Doren might assist in the project, but nothing happened. Tonner then took the manuscript to Carey McWilliams who described the incident this way: "This chap [Tonner, "a kind of 'man Friday' "] once brought to me a manuscript which was a memoir of Grier-son—a very interesting script which I tried without success to get published."[26] Grierson's long-time friend, Shaemas O'Sheel, had only the same story to tell to Tonner in 1931. So Tonner aban-doned this project too.

Grierson was spared the final knowledge that his last two literary efforts—the poetry anthology and his memoirs—failed to get into print. Fortunately he was spared an even more pitiless truth, reported to Tonner by Bragdon, that by 1929 most of his books were out of print, and *The Valley of Shadows* was not even in the New York Public Library!"[27] On the evening of May 29, 1927, Grierson died at the age of seventy-nine. Five days before the twentieth anniversary of Grierson's death Lawrence Waldemar Tonner died.

Certain circumstances surrounding Grierson's death are as un-canny as many of those of his life. Early in the spring of 1927 Zona Gale had written to Grierson that she planned to stay a few days at the Mission Inn where she hoped to visit him. Grierson cordially replied. Miss Gale then wrote that on March 5 both he and Tonner could expect a visit from her and a Mrs. Cochrane, "who, above all people, needs a shaft of music in her life."[28]

Though brief, Zona Gale's visit with Grierson impressed her deeply, and his piano music she could not forget. Distressed to learn later from Frank Miller that Grierson was financially im-poverished, she sent him a check for one hundred dollars on May 24. Shortly after, she learned from Miller that Grierson had died on May 29. She sent a long, poignant letter of condolence to Tonner in which she mentioned "the movement of inner forces'" prompting her on May 24 to send the money. "From the day that I spent the hour with you and Mr. Grierson," she wrote,

"I had the impulse to see if I could in any way make things easier. . . . I sat down to write and to send fifty dollars. As clear as a voice the word came: 'One Hundred,' and I wrote it so."[29] That Grierson was financially needy is indicated by the fact that the Assistance League of Southern California gave some help just prior to his death. The amount, however, did not keep him from pawning one of his last treasures, a gold watch given him by Edward VII.

Zona Gale had written earlier to friends in Los Angeles encouraging them to arrange a benefit dinner to honor Grierson and to raise money for him. This affair, most significantly, was to be realized; and it was at this dinner that Grierson died. Tonner described Grierson's last evening and his last performance this way:

> It was Sunday evening, May twenty-ninth. We had a number of people invited for a musical recital at our home—about thirty. A collection was to be taken up. Mr. Grierson had played a number of his marvelous instantaneous compositions on the piano and had given the company a talk on his experiences and impressions of France and Italy.
>
> He turned to the instrument and announced that the next and last piece of the evening would be an Oriental improvisation, Egyptian in character.
>
> The piece was long, and when it seemed to be finished he sat perfectly still as if resting after the ordeal of this tremendous composition. He often did that, but it lasted too long and I went up to him—he was gone!
>
> His head was only slightly bent forward, as usual in playing, and his hands rested on the keys of the last chord he had touched.
>
> There had not been the slightest warning. He had seemed in usual health (he always had some indigestion), he had eaten well to gain strength for the evening, and he had been smiling and laughing with the company even a few moments before he passed away.[30]

The quiet drama of Grierson's death terminated the short but touching association between him and Zona Gale who, by arranging for the evening recital, had a part in it even from a distance as far away as Portage, Wisconsin. Beset by this fact, she wrote again to Tonner: "I am still thinking every day of my own part in this." Then, in a statement echoing many others

which Grierson had made about mental phenomena, she concluded the letter, "The strange part was my own release in time
to synchronize to the very day with his going—as if something
had now been worked out and fully paid, or ended."[31]

III *Conclusion*

Grierson remarked in his unpublished *Anecdotes and Episodes*
that the public seldom appreciates a genius until he has been
dead at least thirty years. With the re-issue of *The Valley of
Shadows* in 1948, twenty-one years after he died, many reviewers
thought that here was the start of a genuine Grierson revival. In
his editor's note, Bernard DeVoto confidently said that now
Grierson's works "will be better known"—a prediction that has
not come true. Furthermore, the chances are slim that the kind of
appreciation Grierson sought, and that DeVoto said he deserved,
will be realized to the extent either person wished. What accounts
for Grierson's limbo?

Edmund Wilson's explanation in *Patriotic Gore* is provocative.
He said that, even though Grierson was admirably free from
national prejudices as he wrote about Emerson, Wagner, Zola,
and others; even though he distinguished the bold outlines of
what was important and what was not; and even though he
perceived the creative force behind statesmen like Lincoln—yet
Grierson never intimately participated in the culture of his day.
"We are always being stopped on the threshold; we are never
taken inside anything."

This statement is another way of saying that Grierson's difficulty comes in his vacillation. He wavered between escapism
and revolt; between an imaginative retreat from, and an icono-
clastic attack upon, his contemporary world; between dynamic
individualism and staid conservatism; between estheticism and
moral dogmatizing; between the roles of prophet and *poseur;*
and, it must be said, between guile and innocence. Fortunately,
literary history is broad enough to contain all these extremes;
but, when they touch a person's work, then literary criticism
must determine the consequences. With Grierson, it is clear that
had he given wholehearted support to the vital forces of his day
(symbolism in literature, Bergsonian vitalism, depth psychology,
and the like), he would have played a more dominant role in

literary circles. Or had he attacked these forces, or others, with the kind of powerful knowledge which commands authority, his voice would still be echoing today. While it is true, as Van Wyck Brooks said, that Grierson's essays were "slight and airy in their fragile charm," this very quality assured their perishability, especially when behind these essays was a writer who had never really plunged into the shaping forces of his time.

This criticism does not overlook Grierson's own awareness that he was caught in contemporary conflicts, such as the one between science and metaphysics. He saw that in this conflict more was at stake than certain hypotheses of Copernicus, Darwin, or Freud. The fundamental issue was between two *ways* of looking at life—the scientific and the metaphysical. He saw clearly enough that the compromise which eighteenth-century scientists entered into with the philosophers was destined inevitably to give way to a wholly scientific and mechanistic world-view in which the positivists would see in nature nothing more than causal processes and, in mind, nothing more than a minor epiphenomenon of brain and nervous systems. Grierson painfully understood this conflict. Yet his participation in it only sent him bouncing back and forth between Romantic idealism and spiritual science, between religious mystics and California quacks.

The point is not that vacillation itself is weakness. Living as he did between two worlds, one dead and the other powerless to be born, he experienced the same anxieties known to many other thoughtful persons at the turn of the century. His weakness is not in the frustration, not in the lostness or the irresolution, but rather in the belief that somewhere amid all the tangled ambiguities are to be found simple solutions. If only, for example, the middle class showed more cultivated tastes; if only social legislation did away with American night clubs, jazz, and gin; if only the writers discontinued their shocking Realism and turn again toward Romantic beauty; and finally, if only Theosophy or some other cult created a new race of men whose "higher consciousness" would free them from the burden of being only human—here are the "ifs" which Grierson yearned for, and here is his weakness, as it must be the weakness of any writer who thinks that human beings finally can annul their own condition.

But these are matters far beyond the scope of this discussion. What must be said, after all the reservations about Grierson, is that in *The Valley of Shadows* we have a book which does deserve to be better known. This is truly a neglected work in American literature. To repeat or embroider the acclaim already given by DeVoto, Wilson, Roy P. Basler, Carl Sandburg, Theodore Spencer, and others serves no purpose except to underscore the fact that, as America continues to come of age, it will discover an ever more variegated texture to its life. In this discovery, a writer like Francis Grierson will take his rightful place.

Notes and References

Chapter One

1. William Vipond Pooley, *The Settlement of Illinois from 1830 to 1850* (Bulletin of the University of Wisconsin, May, 1908), I, 501-2.
2. *Anecdotes and Episodes* (unpublished MS), pp. 4-5. Unless otherwise noted, all cited unpublished material including letters is to be found in the Leetha Journey Hofeller Collection.
3. Edwin Björkman, *Voices of Tomorrow: Critical Studies of the New Spirit in Literature* (New York, 1913), p. 163.
4. Lawrence Waldemar Tonner to General B. H. Grierson (Nov. 13, 1889), Illinois State Historical Society, hereafter referred to as ISHS.
5. Emily Shepard to General Grierson (Oct. 25, 1865; April 18, 1871; March 4, 1874), ISHS.
6. Edmund Wilson's review of *The Valley of Shadows* in *The New Yorker*, XXIV (Sept. 18, 1948), 106.
7. *Anecdotes and Episodes*, p. 4; *The Valley of Shadows* (Boston and New York, 1909), p. 187.
8. Björkman, p. 162.
9. Wilson, 1948 review, p. 102.
10. Anon., *American Historical Review*, LIV (October, 1948), 163.
11. William W. Sweet, *Religion on the American Frontier*, 4 vols. (University of Chicago Press, 1931, 1936, 1939, 1946); Charles A. Johnson, *The Frontier Camp Meeting: Religion's Harvest Time* (Southern Methodist University Press, 1955); Charles Beneulyn Johnson, *Illinois in the Fifties: A Decade of Development 1851-1860* (Champaign, Illinois, 1918), pp. 68-72.
12. James C. Leyburn, *Frontier Folkways* (Yale University Press, 1935), p. 197.
13. Carl Sandburg, *Abraham Lincoln, The Prairie Years* (New York, 1926), II, 151, 155-56.
14. Roy P. Basler, *The Lincoln Legend: A Study in Changing Conceptions* (Boston, 1935), Chap. iv.
15. *Abraham Lincoln, The Practical Mystic* (New York, 1918), p. 13.
16. *Anecdotes and Episodes*, pp. 8-9.
17. *Ibid.*, p. 10.
18. Emily Shepard to General Grierson (Oct. 25, 1865), ISHS.
19. *Anecdotes and Episodes*, p. 12.
20. Arthur Farwell, "Francis Grierson–Musical Liberator," *Musical America*, XIX (Dec. 13, 1913), 19.
21. Carl Holliday, "Francis Grierson–Mystic," *South Atlantic Quarterly*, XV (October, 1916), 379.
22. Emily Shepard to General Grierson (Oct. 25, 1865), ISHS.
23. *The Celtic Temperament* (London, 1911), pp. viii-ix.

Chapter Two

1. *The Celtic Temperament* (London, 1911), p. viii.
2. "Pen Pictures of Persons and Places, II," *The Golden Era,* XXXVI (December, 1887), 695-700.
3. *The Celtic Temperament,* pp. vii-viii.
4. Grierson quotes H. Henri Delage, a French journalist in attendance, as saying that an American Indian might just as well have been imported "to show the Parisians how a piano should be played" ("My Début in Paris," *Century,* XC [October, 1915], 951).
5. *Ibid.,* p. 952.
6. *Ibid.,* pp. 951-958; "Stéphane Mallarmé," *Poetry, A Magazine of Verse,* II (April-September, 1913), 104-7; "Pen Pictures of Persons and Places," *The Golden Era,* XXXVI (December, 1887), 695-700.
7. Lawrence Waldemar Tonner, *The Genius of Francis Grierson* (Los Angeles, 1927), p. 3; *Anecdotes and Episodes* (unpublished MS), p. 47.
8. "My Visit to Auber," *English Review,* XVIII (September, 1914), 185-86.
9. *Anecdotes and Episodes,* pp. 24-29. Grierson's interview with Dumas is described in Guy Endore's historical novel about Dumas, *King of Paris* (New York, 1956), pp. 85-87.
10. *Parisian Portraits* (London, 1910), p. 32.
11. Emily Shepard to General Grierson (April 18, 1871), ISHS.
12. *Anecdotes and Episodes,* p. 51.
13. Van Wyck Brooks, *The Confident Years 1885-1915* (New York, 1952), pp. 268-69.
14. *Anecdotes and Episodes,* p. 54.
15. *Ibid.,* p. 56.
16. *Ibid.,* pp. 56-57.
17. Arthur Christy (ed.), *The Asian Legacy and American Life* (New York, 1942), p. 44.
18. The account of Grierson's visit at Chittenden comes from his *Anecdotes and Episodes,* pp. 68-73; also from Grierson's letter to Claude Bragdon, printed in the latter's *Merely Players* (New York, 1929), pp. 155-57.
19. Gertrude Williams, *Priestess of the Occult* (New York, 1946), p. 8.
20. Henry Steel Olcott, *Old Diary Leaves: The True Story of the Theosophical Society* (New York, 1895), p. 8.
21. *Ibid.,* pp. 8-9.
22. *Anecdotes and Episodes,* pp. 72-73.
23. Quoted by Olcott, p. 9.
24. *Ibid.,* p. 68.
25. *Ibid.,* p. 68n.
26. *Anecdotes and Episodes,* p. 23.
27. H. C. Hensley, *Early San Diego,* I (unpublished MS in San Diego Public Library), pp. 498-99.
28. *Boston Ideas,* LXIX (April 16, 1928), 8.
29. Franklin Walker, *A Literary History of Southern California* (University of California Press, 1950), p. 100.

30. *San Diego Union* (July 20, 1913), Sec. 2, p. 1. The newspaper reporter interviewed several old citizens who remembered Grierson (Shepard) in San Diego. The account deals chiefly with the Villa Montezuma, a "Weird House of Ghosts This / Built by Spiritualist as Home of Spooks."

31. Mrs. Vine Bowers, "Recollections of Jesse Shepard" (unpublished MS in Serra Junipero Historical Museum, San Diego Historical Society). p. 1. According to Ben Dixon ("Notes on Francis Grierson" [unpublished MS in Serra Junipero Historical Museum]), Mrs. Bowers was a niece of Father Alonzo Horton, founder of modern San Diego.

32. *San Diego Union*, pp. 1, 29.

33. Jesse Shepard to General Grierson (March 15, 1889), ISHS.

34. These accounts come from Bowers and Hensley.

35. *San Diego Union*, p. 29.

36. Jesse Shepard to General Grierson (June 1, 1887), ISHS.

37. L. W. Tonner to General Grierson (Nov. 13, 1889), ISHS.

38. Bowers' MS, p. 4.

Chapter Three

1. Van Wyck Brooks, *Scenes and Portraits* (New York, 1954), p. 230.

2. Edmund Wilson, *Patriotic Gore: Studies in the Literature of the American Civil War* (New York, 1962), p. 77.

3. "The Abbé Roux," *The Golden Era*, XXXVI (June, 1887), 338-43; "Pen Pictures of Persons and Places, I," XXXVI (July, 1887), 401-8; "Imitative Talent versus Creative Faculty," XXXVI (August, 1887), 435-40; "Excerpts from the Writings of Jesse Shepard," XXXVI (October, 1887), 593-95; "Pen Pictures of Persons and Places, II," XXXVI (December, 1887), 695-700; "Pen Pictures of Persons and Places, III," XXXVII (April, 1888), 225-28.

4. *The Golden Era* Library Notes for December, 1887, as quoted by Ben Dixon, "Notes on Francis Grierson," unpublished MS (1953), Serra Junipero Historical Museum, San Diego.

5. "Imitative Talent versus Creative Faculty," *The Golden Era*, XXXVI (August, 1887), 435-40.

6. Facts have been confusing about the publication of this essay. Ernest Sutherland Bates wrote in "Francis Grierson, Prophet of Wonder" (*The Trend* [March, 1914]) that "in 1889 his [Grierson's] first volume appeared, a collection of essays and aphorisms in French entitled 'La Révolte Idéaliste.' " In his account of Grierson written for the *Dictionary of American Biography* (eds. Allen Johnson and Dumas Malone [New York, 1931], VII, 615) he stated again that "La Révolte Idéaliste" was "his first book." Other scholars have made similar references to this "book": see Theodore Spencer's Introduction to *The Valley of Shadows* (fifth edition), pp. xxx-xxxi, and Edmund Wilson's *Patriotic Gore*, p. 74. To the contrary, Grierson stated in *The Celtic Temperament* (p. xiii) that "in that year [1889] I published a book in Paris which contained an essay entitled 'La Révolte Idéaliste.' " The *book* was *Pensées et Essais;* the *essay*, "La Révolte Idéaliste."

7. *Pensées et Essais* (Paris, 1889), pp. 70, 71. Quotes from French are translated by author (HPS).

8. *Essays and Pen-Pictures* (Paris, 1889), p. 79.

9. Mallarmé to Shepard (Dec. 27, 1892).

10. Henri de Bornier to Shepard (Oct. 29, 1890).

11. A copy of this poem is in the Hofeller Collection.

12. Tonner inserted a few short sections in Grierson's *Anecdotes and Episodes;* his description of Gmunden is found on pp. 104-8.

13. *The Spectator*, LXXXII (March 25, 1899), 422.

14. *The Westminster Review*, CLI (June, 1899), 716.

15. Maurice Maeterlinck to Tonner (March 27, 1899).

16. William Sharp to Grierson (May 29, 1899).

17. William James to Grierson (March 19, 1909).

18. Austin Harrison to Grierson (Oct. 12, 1911).

19. Robert H. Davis to Grierson (Sept. 9, 1913).

20. Benjamin De Casseres to Grierson (n.d.).

21. *Critic*, XLII (June, 1903), 462.

22. Quoted by Claude Bragdon, *Merely Players* (New York, 1929), p. 153.

23. Edwin Björkman, *Voices of Tomorrow: Critical Studies of the New Spirit in Literature* (New York, 1913), p. 168.

24. Van Wyck Brooks, *The Confident Years 1885-1915* (New York, 1952), p. 269.

25. Brooks, *Scenes and Portraits*, pp. 229-30.

26. Mary Austin, *Earth Horizon* (Boston, 1932), p. 315.

27. Arnold Bennett, *The Savour of Life, Essays in Gusto* (New York, 1928), p. 239.

28. Bennett, *Journals* (London, 1932), I, 315.

29. *Ibid.*, I, 366.

30. Bennett, *The Savour of Life*, p. 237.

31. Anon., "Francis Grierson, The Prophet of a New Mysticism," *Current Literature*, LII (January, 1912), 76; Boston *Athenaeum*, I (May 24, 1913), 565; New York *Times* (May 25, 1913), 31; *Dial*, LV (July 6, 1913), 56; Boston *Transcript* (April 26, 1913), 6.

32. J. Lewis May, *John Lane and the Nineties* (London, 1936), p. 240.

33. Arthur Farwell, "Francis Grierson–Musical Liberator," *Musical America*, XIX (Dec. 13, 1913), 19.

34. Björkman, "The Music of Francis Grierson," *Harper's Weekly*, LVIII (Feb. 14, 1914), 15.

Chapter Four

1. Anatole France, *La Vie en Fleur* (Paris, 1922), p. 297.

2. "Offenbach and Hortense Schneider," *The English Review*, XIV (March, 1914), 495.

3. Erich Auerbach, *Mimesis: The Representation of Reality in Western Literature*, trans. Willard R. Trask (Princeton University Press, 1953), p. 506.

4. "Stéphane Mallarmé," *Poetry*, II (April-September, 1913), 105.

5. Esme Wingfield-Stratford, *The Victorian Aftermath* (New York, 1934), p. 54.

Notes and References

6. Quoted by William Gaunt. *The Aesthetic Adventure* (New York, 1945), p. 10. Graham Hough, *The Last Romantics* (London, 1949), p. 189, ascribes two meanings to Gautier's dictum: first, "the independence of art from political and social considerations"; second, "the superiority of the formal perfection of art to any other kind of value."

7. G. M. Trevelyan, *English Social History* (New York, 1942), p. 550.

8. R. J. Cruikshank, *Roaring Century 1846-1946* (London, 1946), p. 171.

9. "The Doom of American Democracy," *Westminster Review*, CLVII (May, 1902), 542n.

10. Merle Curti, *The Growth of American Thought* (New York, 1951), Chap. xx.

11. Brooks Adams, *The Law of Civilization and Decay: An Essay on History* (New York, 1896), pp. 381, 383.

12. Gaunt, pp. 45-46.

13. William York Tindall, *Forces in Modern British Literature 1885-1956* (New York, 1956), p. 3.

14. Holbrook Jackson, *The Eighteen Nineties: A Review of Art and Ideas at the Close of the Nineteenth Century* (London, 1913), p. 137.

15. Dixon Wecter, *The Saga of American Society: A Record of Social Aspiration 1607-1937* (New York, 1937), p. 428.

16. "English Fogyism," *Critic*, XLII (June, 1903), 531-34.

17. Alexis de Tocqueville, *Democracy in America*, ed. Henry Steele Commager (New York, 1947), p. 292.

18. Alfred North Whitehead, *Adventures of Ideas* (New York, 1933), pp. 44-45.

19. Bertrand Russell, *Mysticism and Logic* (New York, 1929), p. 57.

Chapter Five

1. John Herman Randall, Jr., *The Making of the Modern Mind*, rev. ed. (New York, 1940), Chaps. xxviii-xxx.

2. *The Humour of the Underman*, p. 25. Wagner's gloom and "labyrinthian pessimism" is treated in "The Wagnerian Riddle" and "Nietzsche and Wagner" in *The Humour of the Underman;* "The Soul's New Refuge" in *The Invincible Alliance;* and "Parsifalitis" in *Modern Mysticism.*

3. Immanuel Kant, *Theory of Ethics*, trans. T. K. Abbott (London, 1889), Bk. 11, Chap. xi, Sec. 6.

4. Randall, p. 599.

5. Claude Bragdon, *Merely Players* (New York, 1929), p. 154.

6. Edmund Wilson, *Patriotic Gore: Studies in the Literature of the American Civil War* (New York, 1962), p. 76.

7. *The Celtic Temperament*, p. 160. The passage is from "The Psychic Action of Genius," the essay William James thought "to be a little 'in the air.'" (William James to Grierson [March 15, 1907].)

8. *Anecdotes and Episodes* (unpublished MS), p. 128.

9. Carl Holliday, "Francis Grierson–Mystic," *South Atlantic Quarterly*, XV (October, 1916), 379.

10. Henry Adams, *The Education* (New York, 1918), p. 485.

11. Percy Bysshe Shelley, *Essays and Letters,* ed. Ernest Rhys (London, 1886), p. 6.

12. A. G. Lehmann, *The Symbolist Aesthetic in France 1885-1895* (Oxford, 1950), p. 63.

13. *Ibid.,* pp. 174-75.

14. Arthur Symons, *The Symbolist Movement in Literature* (London, 1899), pp. 8, 125.

15. Edmund Wilson, *Axel's Castle* (New York, 1931), p. 13.

16. Walter Pater, *Complete Works* (London, 1910), I, 31.

Chapter Six

1. Claude Bernard, *An Introduction to the Study of Experimental Medicine,* trans. Henry Copley Greene (New York, 1949), pp. 12-13, 93.

2. Bernard Weinberg, *French Realism: The Critical Period 1830-1870* (New York, 1937), pp. 118-19.

3. Hippolyte Taine, *The Ideal in Art,* trans. J. Durand (New York, 1870), pp. 27-28.

4. Jacques Maritain, *Creative Intuition in Art and Poetry* (New York, 1953), p. 56.

5. *Ibid.,* p. 56.

6. Quoted by Weinberg, p. 133.

7. See Henri Bergson, *The Creative Mind,* trans. Mabelle L. Andison (New York, 1949), p. 128.

8. A. G. Lehmann, *The Symbolist Aesthetic in France 1885-1895* (Oxford, 1950), p. 106.

9. Albert Beguin, "Poetry and Occultism," *Yale French Studies,* Fourth Issue, Vol. II, 2, pp. 12-17.

10. Max Nordau, *Degeneration* (New York, 1895), p. 227.

11. See *The Celtic Temperament,* pp. 44-52, and *The Humour of the Underman,* pp. 8-10.

12. Samuel Taylor Coleridge, *Complete Works,* ed. W. G. T. Shedd (New York, 1871), V, 55; Walter Pater, *Complete Works* (London, 1910), V, 10.

13. Irwin Edman, *Under Whatever Sky* (New York, 1951), p. 12.

14. *Some Thoughts* (London, 1911), n.p.

15. Springfield *Republican* (May 8, 1913), 5; *Independent,* XCIV (June 22, 1918), 488.

16. Holbrook Jackson, *The Eighteen Nineties: A Review of Art and Ideas at the Close of the Nineteenth Century* (London, 1913), p. 178.

17. Ernest Renan, *The Poetry of the Celtic Races, and Other Studies,* trans. William G. Hutchison (London, Walter Scott Library), p. 2. Renan groups the Celts into four categories: (1) the Welsh and those on the Cornwall peninsula, (2) the dwellers in French Brittany, (3) the Gaels of northern Scotland, (4) the Irish (pp. 4-5n). "Celt" is a "generic name of an ancient people, the bulk of whom inhabited the central and western parts of Europe" (*Encyclopaedia Britannica,* 14th ed., V, 102).

18. Richard Ellmann, *The Identity of Yeats* (London, 1954), pp. 16-17.

19. "Excerpts from the Writings of Jesse Shepard," *The Golden Era,* XXXVI (October, 1887), 594.

20. George Lemaitre, *From Cubism to Surrealism in French Literature* (Harvard University Press, 1941), p. 26.

21. *The Celtic Temperament*, pp. 93-97; *The Humour of the Underman*, p. 54.

Chapter Seven

1. Unless otherwise stated, all page references in the text refer to the 1909 Houghton Mifflin edition of *The Valley of Shadows*.

2. Quoted by Claude Bragdon, *Merely Players* (New York, 1929), p. 153.

3. *The New Yorker*, XXIV (Sept. 18, 1948), 106.

4. New York *Times Book Review* (July 25, 1948), p. 10.

5. *The Literary Digest*, XXXVIII (May 15, 1909), 851.

6. *The Dial*, XLVII (Sept. 16, 1909), 186.

7. A. R. Orage, *The Art of Reading* (New York, 1919), p. 44.

8. *Abraham Lincoln: The Practical Mystic* (New York, 1918), p. 14.

9. *The* (London) *Observer* (Aug. 17, 1912); Boston *Herald* (April 19, 1909); *The* (Glasgow) *Evening News* (April 15, 1909); B. O. Flower, "The Valley of Shadows, A Book Study," *Arena*, XLI (July, 1909), 498-508.

10. New York *Times* (Aug. 21, 1909), p. 2.

11. *New Republic*, LI (July 6, 1927), 172.

12. Mary Austin to Grierson (Aug. 23, 1911).

13. Allen Nevins, *Frémont, The West's Greatest Adventurer* (New York, 1928), II, 556n.

14. New York *Times* (Aug. 21, 1909), p. 2.

15. Samuel Eliot Morison and Henry Steele Commager, *The Growth of the American Republic*, 3rd ed. (New York, 1942), II, 284.

16. Roy P. Basler, *The Lincoln Legend: A Study in Changing Conceptions* (Boston, 1935), pp. 46, 183.

17. Carl Sandburg, *Abraham Lincoln: The Prairie Years* (New York, 1926), II, 151, 155-56.

18. Anon., *American Historical Review*, LIV (October, 1948), 163.

19. Edmund Wilson, *Patriotic Gore: Studies in the Literature of the American Civil War* (New York, 1962), p. 82.

20. See *The Nation*, LXXXVIII (July 10, 1909), 585, for a typical expression of this criticism.

21. In writing these two chapters—"The Pioneer of the Sangamon Country" and "The Regulators"—Grierson may have read J. L. McConnell, *Western Characters or Types of Border Life in the Western States* (New York, 1853), which gives a full account of the Cutler-Roberts-Stone affair (pp. 178-221).

22. Anti-intellectualism among settlers and preachers is noted by many historians of the West. See, for example, James Hall, *Legends of the West* (Philadelphia, 1833), p. 43, and Bayard R. Hall, *The New Purchase, or Early Years in the West* (New Albany, Indiana, 1855), p. 117.

23. See Lincoln's letter to Horace Greeley (Aug. 22, 1862) in *The Collected Works of Abraham Lincoln*, ed. Roy P. Basler (Rutgers University Press, 1953), V, 388.

24. David Donald, *Lincoln Reconsidered: Essays on the Civil War Era* (New York, 1956), p. 27.

25. Sandburg, *The Prairie Years*, II, 101.

26. See Charles Beneulyn Johnson, *Illinois in the Fifties, or A Decade of Development 1851-1860* (Champaign, 1918), pp. 68-70; William W. Sweet, *Revivalism in America: Its Origin and Decline* (New York, 1944), Chap. vi.

27. Edmund Wilson, "Abraham Lincoln: The Union as Religious Mysticism," in *Eight Essays* (New York, 1954), p. 189.

28. See David Donald, Chap. iv; Richard Hofstadter, *The American Political Tradition* (New York, 1949), Chap. v.

29. See Allan Nevins, *The Statesmanship of the Civil War* (New York, 1953), pp. 59-60; Morison and Commager, I, 634; Theodore Calvin Pease, *The Story of Illinois*, rev. ed. (University of Chicago Press, 1949), p. 168.

30. Dixon Wecter, *The Hero in America: A Chronicle of Hero-Worship* (New York, 1941), p. 225.

31. *The Collected Works of Abraham Lincoln*, III, 315.

32. *Ibid.*, pp. 318-25.

33. Wilson, *Eight Essays*, p. 189; Sandburg, II, 151.

34. Jay Monaghan, *Civil War on the Western Border 1854-1865* (Boston, 1955), p. 148.

35. John S. Wise, *The End of an Era* (Boston, 1900), p. 168.

36. *Abraham Lincoln, The Practical Mystic* (New York, 1918), p. 9.

37. Wilson, review in *The New Yorker*, p. 102; *Patriotic Gore*, p. 78.

38. Quoted by Bragdon, *Merely Players*, p. 153.

39. DeVoto's Note, *The Valley of Shadows* (fifth edition), p. xvi.

Chapter Eight

1. Quoted by Edmund Wilson, *Patriotic Gore: Studies in the Literature of the American Civil War* (New York, 1962), p. 78.

2. Arthur Farwell, "Francis Grierson—Musical Liberator," *Musical America*, XIX (Dec. 13, 1913), 19.

3. Anon., "The Visit of Francis Grierson," *Current Opinion*, LVI (February, 1914), 135; Ernest Sutherland Bates, "Francis Grierson, Prophet of Wonder," *The Trend* (March, 1914), n.p.; Edwin Björkman, "The Music of Francis Grierson," *Harper's Weekly*, LVIII (Feb. 14, 1914), 15; Carl Holliday, "Francis Grierson—Mystic," *South Atlantic Quarterly*, XV (October, 1916), 379-83.

4. Quoted by Claude Bragdon, *Merely Players* (New York, 1929), p. 149.

5. Eric Goldman, *Rendezvous with Destiny: A History of Modern American Reform*, rev. ed. (New York, 1956), p. 174.

6. Harold E. Stearns, *America, A Re-Appraisal* (New York, 1937), pp. 292-93.

7. Van Wyck Brooks, *Days of the Phoenix: The Nineteen Twenties I Remember* (New York, 1957), p. 43.

8. See *The Outlook*, CXXI (Jan. 22, 1919), 160; *Athenaeum* (Nov. 28, 1919), 1274; Springfield *Republican* (Feb. 6, 1919), 8.

9. *The Dial*, LXVII (July 26, 1919), 72.

10. Mary Austin to Tonner (Oct. 5, 1919).

Notes and References

11. Margaret McMillan to Grierson (Oct. 17, 1919), HPS.

12. Quoted by Franklin Walker, *A Literary History of Southern California* (University of California Press, 1950), pp. 257-58.

13. Quoted by Frederick J. Hoffman, *The Twenties: American Writing in the Postwar Decade* (New York, 1955), p. 282.

14. Mary Baker Eddy, *Science and Health with Key to the Scriptures* (Boston, n.d.), p. 468.

15. Hoffman, p. 291.

16. *Religious Bodies: 1926* (Washington D.C., Government Printing Office, 1930), pp. 457-59; *Los Angeles, A Guide to the City and Its Environs,* American Guide Series (New York, 1941), pp. 68-73.

17. P. D. Ouspensky, *Tertium Organum: A Key to the Enigmas of the World,* trans. Nicholas Bessaraboff and Claude Bragdon (New York, 1922), p. 312.

18. *The Diary and Sundry Observations of Thomas Alva Edison,* ed. Dagobert D. Runes (New York, 1948), p. 205.

19. *Ibid.,* pp. 239-40.

20. New York *Times* (Aug. 31, 1926), 10.

21. See the chapter entitled "Dead Authors" in Agnes Repplier, *Points of Fiction* (Boston, 1920), pp. 31-69.

22. George Santayana, *Characters and Opinion in the United States* (New York, 1956), p. 117.

23. Van Wyck Brooks to Tonner (June 20, 1927).

24. Mary Austin to Tonner (July 11, 1927).

25. John Mantle Clapp to Tonner (March 6, 1929).

26. Carey McWilliams to HPS (Dec. 30, 1955).

27. Claude Bragdon to Tonner (July 18, 1929).

28. Zona Gale to Tonner (Feb. 28, 1927), HPS.

29. Zona Gale to Tonner (June 7, 1927), HPS.

30. *Boston Ideas* (Oct. 1, 1927), p. 11.

31. Zona Gale to Tonner (June 15, 1927), HPS.

Selected Bibliography

With the exception of *The Valley of Shadows*, fifth edition (Houghton Mifflin, 1948), all of Francis Grierson's published books are out of print. The main repositories of unpublished material—letters, memorabilia, and manuscripts—are the Leetha Journey Hofeller Collection and the Illinois State Historical Society.

PRIMARY SOURCES

1. Books (first editions)

Essays and Pen-Pictures. Paris: T. Symonds, 1889.

Pensées et Essais. Paris: Librairie Documentaire, 1889.

Modern Mysticism and Other Essays. London: George Allen, 1899.

The Celtic Temperament and Other Essays. London: George Allen, 1901.

The Valley of Shadows. London: John Lane, 1909.

Parisian Portraits. London: Stephen Swift, 1910.

La Vie et les Hommes. London: Stephen Swift, 1911.

Some Thoughts. London: Stephen Swift, 1911.

The Humour of the Underman, and Other Essays. London: Stephen Swift, 1911.

The Invincible Alliance, and Other Essays, Political, Social, and Literary. London: John Lane, 1913.

Illusions and Realities of the War. New York: John Lane, 1918.

Abraham Lincoln, The Practical Mystic. New York: John Lane, 1918.

Psycho-Phone Messages. Los Angeles: Austin Publishing Co., 1921.

2. Articles (not collected in books cited above)

"The Abbé Roux," *The Golden Era*, XXXVI (June, 1887), 338-43.

"Pen Pictures of Persons and Places, I," *The Golden Era*, XXXVI (July, 1887), 401-8.

"Imitative Talent Versus Creative Faculty," *The Golden Era*, XXXVI (August, 1887), 436-40.

"Excerpts from the Writings of Jesse Shepard," *The Golden Era*, XXXVI (October, 1887), 593-95.

"Pen Pictures of Persons and Places, II," *The Golden Era*, XXXVI (December, 1887), 695-700.

"Pen Pictures of Persons and Places, III," *The Golden Era*, XXXVII (April, 1888), 225-28.

"The Blunders of Matthew Arnold," *Westminster Review*, CLVII (March, 1902), 300-6.

"The Doom of American Democracy," *Westminster Review*, CLVII (May, 1902), 519-26.

"English Fogyism," *The Critic*, XLII (June, 1903), 531-34.

"Offenbach and Hortense Schneider," *The English Review*, XVI (March, 1914), 495-503.

Selected Bibliography

"My Visit to Auber," *The English Review,* XVIII (September, 1914), 173-86.
"What Will the War Bring to America?" *Craftsman,* XXVII (November, 1914), 145-49.
"Stéphane Mallarmé," *Poetry, A Magazine of Verse,* II (April-September, 1913), 104-7.

SECONDARY SOURCES

ANON. "Sketch of Grierson," *Critic,* XLII (June, 1903), 492-94. Prediction of Grierson's success as a writer.
——. "Francis Grierson, A Prophet of a New Mysticism," *Current Literature,* LII (January, 1912), 76-78. Announcement that interest in Grierson is spreading in U. S.
——. "The Visit of Francis Grierson," *Current Opinion,* LVI (February, 1914), 135. Brief but enthusiastic sketch.
——. "Weird House of Ghosts This," San Diego *Union* (July 20, 1913), Sec. 2, p. 1. Indispensable account of Grierson's Villa Montezuma and his dealings with the High brothers.
AUSTIN, MARY. *Earth Horizon.* Boston: Houghton Mifflin Co., 1932. Brief references to Grierson's life in London prior to his writing *The Valley of Shadows.*
BAKER, NAOMI. "Villa Montezuma," San Diego *Tribune-Sun* (Oct. 22, 1948), Sec. B, p. 1. Description of the Villa.
BASLER, ROY P. *The Lincoln Legend: A Study in Changing Conceptions.* Boston: Houghton Mifflin Co., 1935. High praise of *The Valley of Shadows* as an interpretation of Lincoln, the mystic.
BATES, ERNEST SUTHERLAND. "Francis Grierson, Prophet of Wonder," *The Trend* (March, 1914). Enthusiastic survey of Grierson's career.
BENNETT, ARNOLD. *The Savour of Life, Essays in Gusto.* New York: Doubleday, Doran and Co., 1928.
——. *Journals.* London: Cassell & Co., Ltd., 1932. Casual dismissal of Grierson as puzzling but second-rate writer and musician.
BJÖRKMAN, EDWIN. "Francis Grierson, A Study in Modern Mysticism," *Forum,* XLVIII (August, 1912), 145-58; "The Music of Francis Grierson," *Harper's Weekly,* LVIII (Feb. 14, 1914), 15. Written by an early student of Grierson's career, both articles contain invaluable commentary (the second gives an excellent description of a Grierson musicale).
——. *Voices of To-Morrow: Critical Studies of the New Spirit in Literature.* New York: Mitchell Kennerley, 1913. Analysis of Grierson's writing (compared with Maeterlinck's and Bergson's).
BOWERS, VINE. "Recollections of Jesse Shepard," unpublished MS (n.d.), San Diego Historical Society, pp. 1-6. Highly amusing, articulate account of Grierson in San Diego.
BRAGDON, CLAUDE. *Merely Players.* New York: Alfred A. Knopf, 1929. Quotations from correspondence to Bragdon; facts about Grierson and Madame Blavatsky at Chittenden, Vermont.
BROOKS, VAN WYCK. *The Confident Years, 1885-1915.* New York: E. P. Dutton, 1952.

———. *Scenes and Portraits.* New York: E. P. Dutton, 1954. Highly urbane reminiscences of visits with Grierson in London.

BULLARD, F. LAURISTON. "The Valley of Shadows," *American Historical Review*, LIV (October, 1948), 163-64. Brief but serious effort to assess Grierson's book in relation to Civil War literature.

DEVOTO, BERNARD. Editor's Note. *The Valley of Shadows.* Fifth edition. Boston: Houghton Mifflin Co., 1948. Deep conviction of book's unique place in American literature.

Dictionary of American Biography (New York, 1931), vol. 7.

DIXON, BEN. "Notes on Francis Grierson," unpublished MS (1953), San Diego Historical Society. Information about Grierson and the Villa Montezuma.

ENDORE, GUY. *King of Paris.* New York: Simon and Schuster, 1956. Novel about Alexander Dumas with interesting references to Grierson.

FARWELL, ARTHUR. "Francis Grierson–Musical Liberator," *Musical America*, XIX (Dec. 13, 1913), 19. Important appraisal of Grierson's music, and welcome upon his return to U.S.

FLOWER, B. O. "The Valley of Shadows, A Book Study," *Arena*, XLI (July, 1909), 498-508. A more than perfunctory effort to assess the book's literary quality.

HENSLEY, H. C. *Early San Diego*, unpublished MS (n.d.), vol. 1, San Diego Public Library. Account of Grierson's Spiritualist practices in both Chicago and San Diego.

HOLLIDAY, CARL. "Francis Grierson–Mystic," *South Atlantic Quarterly*, XV (October, 1916), 379-83. Ponderous evaluation of Grierson's thought.

LEISY, ERNEST E. *The American Historical Novel.* Norman: University of Oklahoma Press, 1950. Routine references to *The Valley of Shadows.*

LEWIS, LLOYD. "The Valley of Shadows," New York *Times Book Review* (July 25, 1948), p. 10. Assertion that the book deserved revival long ago.

MAY, J. LEWIS. *John Lane and the Nineties.* London: John Lane Bodley Head, 1936. Description of one of Grierson's piano recitals and its haunting effect upon Lane.

MORISON, SAMUEL ELIOT and COMMAGER, HENRY STEELE. *The Growth of the American Republic.* New York: Oxford University Press, 1942. Uncritical appraisal of Grierson as a Middle West realist.

OLCOTT, HENRY STEEL. *Old Diary Leaves, The True Story of the Theosophical Society.* New York: G. P. Putnam's Sons, 1895. Important source of information about Grierson and Madame Blavatsky at Chittenden, Vermont.

ORAGE, A. R. *The Art of Reading.* New York: Farrar and Rinehart, Inc., 1930. Plea for a full assessment of Grierson who, to Orage, was a strange combination of writer and charlatan.

O'SHEEL, SHAEMAS. "A Note on the Death of Francis Grierson," *The New Republic*, LI (July 6, 1927), 169-72. A poignant tribute by one of Grierson's friends and most appreciative readers.

SANDBURG, CARL. *Abraham Lincoln, The Prairie Years*, vol. 2. New York: Harcourt Brace and Co., 1926. Sensitive appreciation of Grierson's literary portrait of Lincoln in *The Valley of Shadows.*

Selected Bibliography

SIMONSON, HAROLD P. "Zona Gale's Acquaintance with Francis Grierson," *The Historical Society of Southern California Quarterly*, XLI (March, 1959), 11-16.

————. "Francis Grierson in San Diego: An Episode in Charlatanry," *American Quarterly*, XII (Summer, 1960), 198-204.

————. "Francis Grierson's *The Valley of Shadows*," *Midwest Review* (Spring. 1961), 41-52.

————. "Francis Grierson—A Biographical Sketch and Bibliography," *Journal of the Illinois State Historical Society*, LIV (Summer, 1961), 198-203.

SPENCER, THEODORE. Introduction, *The Valley of Shadows*. Fifth edition. Boston: Houghton Mifflin Co., 1948. Informative introduction to the life and career of Francis Grierson.

TONNER, LAWRENCE WALDEMAR. "Francis Grierson," *Boston Ideas* (Oct. 1, 1927 and April 16, 1938), 8, 11. Account of Grierson's last recital and his death; highly evasive explanation of Grierson's dealings in San Diego.

————. *The Genius of Francis Grierson*. Los Angeles: privately printed, 1927. A pamphlet-size, eulogistic summary of Grierson's career.

VAN DYKE, T. S. *The City and County of San Diego*. San Diego: Leberthon & Taylor, 1888. Contains one of best descriptions of the Villa Montezuma.

WILSON, EDMUND. "The Valley of Shadows," *The New Yorker*, XXIV (Sept. 18, 1948), 101-7. Sharply incisive review of the book's fifth edition.

————. "Abraham Lincoln: The Union as Religious Mysticism," *Eight Essays*. New York: Doubleday and Co., 1954. The Lincoln mystique in Grierson's writing.

————. *Patriotic Gore: Studies in the Literature of the American Civil War*. New York: Oxford University Press, 1962. Informative and gracefully written analysis of Grierson's contribution to Civil War literature.

Index

Swinburne, Algernon, 60, 64
Symons, Arthur, 60

Taine, Hippolyte, 56, 88, 89-90
Tate, Allen, 90
Taylor, Zachary, 21
Teasdale, Sara, 135
Teleki, Michael Albert, 135
Teleki, Countess Rose, 135
Thomson, James, 71
Thoreau, Henry David, 96, 111
Tillich, Paul, 72
Tindall, William York, 65
Tocqueville, Alexis de, 64, 68
Tolstoy, Leo, 67, 96
Tonner, Lawrence Waldemar, 16, 35, 36, 37, 38, 39, 45, 122-23, 132-33, 134-37
Trevelyan, G. M., 61
Troubetskoi, Princess Sophia, 27
Tuttle, Hudson, 33, 34
Twain, Mark, 17, 18, 38, 63, 66, 102, 103

Uncle Remus, 17, 53

Van Doren, Carl, 136
Van Doren, Mark, 135
Van Dyke, Henry, 109
Van Dyke, T. S., 37
Verlaine, Paul, 102

Victoria, Queen, 56, 62
Villa Montezuma, 34-39, 57, 59

Wade, Benjamin, 133
Wagner, Richard, 74-75, 138
Walker, Franklin, 35
Waterman, Robert W., 35
Waugh, Evelyn, 128
Webster, Daniel, 133
Wecter, Dixon, 66, 118
Wells, H. G., 51, 64
Wendell, Barrett, 103
Werfel, Franz, 128
Wharton, Edith, 63
Whitefield, George, 19
Whitehead, Alfred North, 71, 129
Whitman, Walt, 21, 102, 103, 104, 118, 131, 132
Wilde, Oscar, 42, 60, 65, 93. 97
Wilson, Edmund, 15, 17, 19, 35, 40, 43, 78, 87, 105, 109-10, 118, 120, 138, 140
Wilson, Woodrow, 124, 133
Woodbury, George E., 103
Woolf, Virginia, 91
Wright, Frank Lloyd, 125

Yeats, William Butler, 30, 71, 100

Zola, Emile, 28, 41, 42, 56, 58, 90, 92, 94, 138
